YOUR DREAM INSTRUMENT

An Insider's Guide to Buying
Violins, Violas, Cellos, Basses & Bows

EDITED BY
MEGAN WESTBERG

STRING LETTER PUBLISHING

BACK
STAGE
BOOKS

EXCLUSIVELY DISTRIBUTED BY
HAL•LEONARD®

Publisher: David A. Lusterman
Strings Group Publisher: Jenna Burrow
Editorial Director: Greg Cahill
Editor: Megan Westberg
Director of Production and Book Publishing: Ellen Richman
Designers: Timothy Jang, Norma Tennis

Contents (c) 2008 by String Letter Publishing, Inc.
David A. Lusterman, Publisher
ISBN 978-1-890490-99-7

Cover Design: Timothy Jang
Cover image courtesy: Ifshin Violins in Berkeley, California: violin, Gaetano Sgarabotto, Vincenza, Italy, 1927
Cover Photo: Michael Amsler

PO Box 767, San Anselmo, California 94979
(415) 485-6946; www.stringletter.com

Library of Congress Cataloging-in-Publication Data
    Your dream instrument : an insider's guide to buying violins, violas, cellos, basses,
    and bows / edited by Megan Westberg.
        p. cm.
    Includes index.
    ISBN-13: 978-1-890490-99-7 (pbk.)
    ISBN-10: 1-890490-99-7 (pbk.)
    1. Bowed stringed instruments—Purchasing. 2. Stringed instrument bows—
    Purchasing. 3. Bowed stringed instruments—Equipment and supplies—Purchasing.
    I. Westberg, Megan, 1980-
        ML750.Y68 2008
        787'.1922—dc22
                            2008003509

Contents

BUYING BOWS

BUYING ACCESSORIES

Introduction

To most newcomers, the violin trade comes cloaked in mystery. It is a history told in nicks and scratches, in worn varnish and ancient labels. To look at a violin is to not only wonder about the stories it could tell now, but also the stories it will tell later, once your moment in its history is long past.

But upon walking into a violin shop or auction for the first time, the sense of mystery takes on a different, and sometimes overwhelming, form. How does one choose the right stringed instrument, bow, and myriad accessories that line the walls? The editors of *Strings* magazine have compiled this volume to help guide you to your dream instrument or bow.

Here, you'll find the process demystified by experts in the field. Whether you're buying your first instrument, stepping up in quality, interested in commissioning an instrument, or curious about the auction market, you'll find helpful tips and in-depth discussions that can steer you in the right direction.

The antique instrument section offers an auction primer, advice on lesser-known historical makers whose work may prove a good investment at auction, tips on finding an appraiser, a discussion of the value of cultivating a good relationship with a violin shop, and more.

Contemporary makers offer everything from entry-level outfits to professional-quality instruments. These instruments are made in a variety of situations, which accounts for the wide range in quality. The contemporary instrument section provides a view into the exceptional work and great value available in new instruments.

In order to enjoy the beauty of your new instrument's voice, you're going to need a bow. The third section of this volume discusses finding that perfect companion to your instrument.

Finally, you'll need some accessories. Refer to the final section for advice on cases and the importance of finding a chin rest that fits you well.

This book should provide you with much of the information you need to make informed choices. Remember that finding your dream instrument or bow can be a long process. Be patient: the effort you expend is well worth it in the end. Once you find it, there's no telling where the right instrument will take you.

—MEGAN WESTBERG

Section 1

Buying Antique Instruments

CHAPTER 1

Market Forces

Looking for a bargain-basement violin by an old Italian master?
Here are a few tips on getting a good deal on a sound investment

BY PHILIP J. KASS

Oh, for a crystal ball. With auction records shattering right and left, it's tempting to dream of the possible profits if only we could gaze into the future. May of 2006 saw the astonishing $3.5 million achieved by the "Hammer" Stradivari at Christie's. But it isn't just the household names making big news. The Hammer's smashing price was followed in October by the remarkable $486,400 paid for a 1774 viola by the somewhat lesser-known Tommaso Balestrieri, also at Christie's. Tarisio's November 2006 sale established a new record for Gennaro Gagliano at $201,500 (nearly $50,000 higher than the previous record) and doubled the records for violins by Carlo Ferdinando Landolfi and Paolo Antonio Testore set just two years earlier.

A lot of people watched, remembering the prices formerly commanded by those lesser-known makers' instruments, and wondered: Why didn't I buy one of those last year?

Alas, we mere mortals have only the gift of hindsight. However, with some effort, musicians can learn to develop strategies for finding something good at a good price, and potentially make a good investment. Before you begin that process, keep in mind that the search for a good investment is different from the search for a "soul mate."

DEAL OR NO DEAL

As impressive as the public auction records are, private sales have long since surpassed those prices. While Balestrieri, for example, may have been off the average buyer's radar, he had not been overlooked by the dealers.

How did they know, you may ask? Dealers have an understanding of the nature of the market and how violins are priced, reinforced by years of hindsight.

Dealers created the modern stringed-instrument market centuries ago when the first violin makers and musicians began reselling used violins. They developed the expertise to identify authentic examples of individual makers and lutherie schools by discerning recognizable characteristics in style, building technique, and materials. Authenticity is crucial in the pricing of any collectible. As the violin is a user collectible, dealers have traditionally sought to use their expertise to serve a primary clientele of players.

The market that dealers so assiduously study is small. The several thousand instruments sold each year at auction seem like a lot, but they're a drop in the bucket compared to the art world as a whole. Monet created more paintings on

---

⤳ THE BIG PAYOFF ⤳

The antique violin market has always been a bit unpredictable, but odds are that if you buy a good fiddle and keep it long enough, it will appreciate in value for a healthy payoff.

There are some easy ways of guessing what will probably be in demand in the years to come. One certainly cannot go entirely wrong by sticking to the old-Italian formula.

As our definition of "old" keeps changing, so does the available body of work that fits that description.

Another way to identify a good buy is to observe what players are praising. Always keep in mind that there might well be self-interest in that praise. Makers or schools of makers that gain coverage in the press or in books also usually experience a burst of interest and value.

Lastly, one can keep an eye out for what has been overlooked, those instruments whose value relative to other schools seems low.

Do the math: when the market price of one maker has not appeared to keep pace with the work of another maker whose instruments are a substitute, there is room for quick appreciation. They might well have a rosy future ahead of them.

My personal favorites in the "rosy future" class have long been the English and American schools, and I am sure that eventually I'll be vindicated. My belief is that older American instruments have long been undervalued and overlooked, and that hard-pressed musicians can gain great utility from them at a very reasonable price. Those instruments began appreciating about the time Thomas James

holiday in Venice than most classic Italian masters created in a lifetime. The dollar amount of last year's violin sales is almost invisible to the financial world, where a slow day on Wall Street involves the trade of several billion dollars.

So, with relatively little to trade, expert violin dealers have long dominated the market for the finest examples by just about every maker. What was left over—because it wasn't particularly desirable, had problems of condition or authenticity, or just wasn't needed—went to the public auctions.

Auctions have traditionally functioned as an open wholesale market, but this began to change in 1971 when Sotheby's offered the 1721 "Lady Blunt" Stradivari. At the time, it was one of the very finest examples in private hands. The near-retail selling price, just over $200,000, sent a shockwave through the market. But even then the "Lady Blunt" sold for less than it would have from a dealer.

Dealers can charge more and get it because of the generally better quality of their stock, usually offered in fully restored state and with at least adequate documentation, and the potential liability incurred if their opinion on attribution is wrong. As violin expert and dealer Robert Bein once wrote, "The opinions that I formulate are translated into financial guarantees that are in force for the life of the business." Other dealer amenities such as the availability of service after the sale, including maintenance of a full-service shop, add to the price tag. But not having

---

Wenberg's 1986 book, *The Violin Makers of the United States*, was published. Some of the best makers, such as the Whites of Boston and the Gemunders of New York, have already experienced growth over the past few decades.

But they are just the tip of the iceberg.

The best of the English makers have also gained in value. Cellists have long known the fine work of the Forsters, Thomas Dodd, Thomas Kennedy, and Benjamin Banks. Vincent Panormo and John Lott are legendary and have been among the price leaders of that school. Often overlooked, though, are some of their contem-poraries, such as the Fendt family and Lockey Hill. Among more modern English makers, there is already strong admiration for the work of George Wulme-Hudson, William Luff, and the Vollers, who were notoriously implicated in the manufacture of fakes.

There has not been an exceptional Voller instrument at auction for a while, at least not one catalogued as such, but in light of the recently published book *The Voller Brothers* (British Violin Making Association, 2006) the next occurrence could prove quite a surprise.

—P.J.K.

> **My personal favorites in the "rosy future" class have long been the English and American schools**

these facilities does not mean that small-time or private dealers charge less—they often charge more in my experience.

WHEEL OF FORTUNE

It takes time, something very few musicians have, to develop the expertise to recognize a sleeper at auction, pick it up cheap, and turn it around for a speedy profit. But musicians can develop the other tactics: listening to chatter among players and dealers, following private and public pricing, and learning enough about violin history to figure out who might be comparable but underpriced makers.

When word of mouth focuses on a specific set of makers who offer great value or great sound, both buyers and sellers become name conscious. Since limited production and a minuscule resale volume keep the supply of any one maker's work scarce, the higher expectations of sellers and popular demand among buyers work together to raise prices. As prices rise, buyers begin to pay attention to the work of other makers whose origins, quality, and value have historically been comparable. The result is that, as the value of one maker rises, so does the comparative value of his contemporaries and peers, as buyers seek alternatives to what is unavailable.

WHERE THE PRICE IS RIGHT

For investment purposes, one can't go wrong with an old Italian. Over the last 30 years, most fine French instruments have appreciated tenfold, while the better-known Italian names (leaving out Strad and Guarneri) have gone up 15-fold or more. If a $400,000 Balestrieri is out of your price range, what else would be comparable to Balestrieri, i.e. Italian and of the same general age? Lorenzo Storioni, G.B. Ceruti, and Giuseppe Guadagnini spring to mind. If these are out of range, a step down yields, among others, the best works of the Gaglianos (which have seen a lot of action recently on the auction block), Anselmo Bellosio, and Michele Deconetti of Venice; C.F. Landolfi and Pietro Mantegazza of Milan; and Camillo Camilli of Mantua, most likely Balestrieri's teacher.

Among 19th-century Italian makers we have G.F. Pressenda, G.A. Rocca, and Allesandro D'Espine of Turin; and Enrico Ceruti of Cremona. These are usually not as

> The less fashionable schools deliver more instrument for the money, and aren't necessarily a bad investment.

expensive, although the Turin makers have been in high demand for some years and so the gap has narrowed.

Vis-à-vis tone quality and workmanship, the less fashionable schools deliver more instrument for the money, and aren't necessarily a bad investment. For example, when I started in the violin-dealing business in 1977, a J.B. Vuillaume sold for about $15,000. When I left the violin-dealing trade in 2002, Vuillaumes were selling for $150,000. Still a relative bargain. French fiddles are not as highly valued simply because they deprive their owners of the cachet of saying, "I have an Italian violin."

An exquisite violin by Nicholas Lupot, the finest of the French makers, was offered last spring with an estimate of $175,000 to $200,000. It didn't sell because the thinking was, "For just a little more money I can get an Italian." A third-rate Italian . . . but an Italian.

French-made violins by Georges Chanot, who was very much Vuillaume's equal, sell now at $70,000 to $80,000, half Vuillaume's price and double what they were selling for in 1998. At the next level down are works of French luthiers Honore Derazey, the brothers Silvestre, Nicolas François Vuillaume of Brussels, and the Gands and Bernardels, all of first-class quality but with much lower price tags.

First figure out what you really like: do you prefer French fiddles? Modern Italian? English cellos? Then look for the lesser-known makers working at the same time or in the same place until you come to the intersection of what you like and what you can afford.

THE KRYPTON FACTORS

So, off we go, searching for an investment we can use to play Beethoven. First start with the tone, right? Wrong, at least in terms of making a good financial decision. Tone is variable. Even with the greatest concert violins, where there seems to be unanimity of agreement on their tone, it is still a matter of opinion. To establish real investment grade in an instrument, one needs some absolutes, the same absolutes experts and dealers use in judging an instrument: authenticity, provenance, and condition.

Authenticity always comes first. What sense is there in buying a fake for the price of the genuine article? When it comes to resale, the seller ought to be able to confirm that the instrument in question was made by a given maker and that there is general agreement on who it is.

In spite of how it sometimes seems, there is general agreement on authenticity for a great deal of the known instruments. When a luthier learns to make violins, he (and only very rarely she) learns certain traditions and forms certain habits of construction. These things, once learned, are changed only when convenience or improvement suggests another approach. Thus, style becomes regular and predictable, and readily identifiable to those familiar with it.

While authenticity provides the basis for an instrument's worth, provenance adds extra sizzle. It is essentially a clear history of the instrument and a record of past ownership that confirms that an old violin wasn't made yesterday. Past certificates of authenticity are often the proof, provided they truly accompany the instrument they describe. However, sometimes those past owners themselves can

---

∽ TIC-TAC DOUGH ∾

To understand the relationship between auction and private pricing, let's take a closer look at the case of Balestrieri, who worked from about 1750 to 1788 in Mantua. Based on recent auction results, the value of his instruments appears to have skyrocketed: November 2005 saw a new record of $232,850 set at Bongartz, a significant increase over the old record of $168,845 set in 2002. In February 2006, Sotheby's set still another record at $402,680 and Christie's commanded $486,400 for a viola in October 2006. The three sold at auction since November 2005 have been standouts in terms of quality and condition, two important determinants of value, and their prices have been impressive.

The viola generated particular interest because old Italian violas are scarce as hens' teeth and to offer one in exceptional condition and an ideal playing size was a real coup for the auctioneer.

It's tempting to look at those results and wonder why. Over this same period there have been at least as many Balestrieris in the hands of dealers worldwide; their prices, while private and confidential after the sale, are public information while they are being offered. My experience over the last few years has been that prices have been at or above the highest figures realized at auction. Basically, the combination of limited production and an inflexible market has meant that demand has always exceeded supply.

If you go to a few dealers and they have nice, healthy, well-documented Balestrieris for the going prices, and one shows up at the auctions in questionable shape, needing restoration, without any papers, and without the seller really being accountable, will the sensible buyer pay retail?

And so, you see wholesale or speculative low-ball offers at the auctions, and retails at the dealers. Then an auction gets a "creampuff," and all bets are off. A few retail buyers, hoping for a bargain, get into a bidding war and drive the price to (almost but not quite, usually) retail, and everyone who hasn't been paying attention to comparative prices gets pulled up short. Remember that auctions offer instruments as is, something most quality shops can't get away with. No spikes were involved here, simply a gradual rise accelerated by erratic availability and variable physical condition. This involves no change in other makers' works as their supply picture remains the same. The sharp buyer might use the newly posted results as a basis of comparison, go out scouting comparable makers' works in comparable state vis-à-vis condition and documentation, and hope to catch one out there that has been accidentally priced low. That presumes a dealer who doesn't watch the market, so good luck.

—P.J.K.

add significant interest and value to an instrument. Violins used by Paganini, Kreisler, and Heifetz carry significant value above and beyond their intrinsic worth.

Lastly, condition plays a key role in both the value and the desirability of an instrument. A beaten-up fiddle should never have as much value as a well-cared-for, fresh example. A beaten-up fiddle often has structural problems that repairs can never entirely correct, so a violin with significant damage can be unreliable. Dealers will not be attracted to a badly damaged instrument unless its problems are offset by significant qualities, such as beauty, documentation, and a very cheap price—and even then, they know that a lot of explaining will have to be done to resell it.

After all these considerations have been acknowledged, take a bow to the instrument and hear whether its sound appeals to you. Will it do what you need? Is it good enough? Sometimes, good enough is just that. It is the rare player who keeps an instrument for an entire career. Tastes change over a lifetime. If you've bought according to the three aforementioned absolutes, rather than buying a noble wreck of dubious parentage simply because it sounded good, you will find that there are more lined up to buy it when the day comes that you want to sell it.

A version of this chapter originally appeared in the June/July 2007 issue of Strings *magazine.*

CHAPTER 2

Tips on Finding an Appraiser

Guidelines for the appraisal process

BY JAMES N. McKEAN

The annual *Strings* Buyer's Guide lists scores of expert appraisers. You can also search our online database at www.stringsmagazine.com, or contact a reputable trade organization to find an appraiser in your area. There are a few things you should know before asking someone to estimate the value of your stringed instrument, however. Here are five guidelines:

SELECTING AN APPRAISER

Choosing a qualified appraiser is not always a simple process. It's easier to find appraisers in metropolitan areas than in rural ones. Instrument appraisers may also be instrument dealers or makers, or they may be employed at auction houses.

When approaching a dealer for an appraisal, look for one with a repair department or one trained in repair techniques—he or she will be most apt to recognize condition issues that may affect the value of your instrument. Auction houses with active musical-instrument departments are often a great source of expertise. Their appraisal departments are well equipped to supply appraisals that will stand up to the closest scrutiny.

If you live in a region with no knowledgeable appraisers, you'll probably need to go outside your area. If this is the case, start the process by sending photographs first and then shipping the piece to the appraiser. It is always advisable to select an appraiser who is a member of a professional lutherie organization such as the Violin Society of America (VSA; www.vsa.to) or American Federation of Violin and Bow Makers (AFVBM; www.afvbm.com), or a professional appraisal organization, such as the Appraisers Association of America (www.appraisersassoc.org).

TYPES OF APPRAISALS

Verbal If you're simply curious about the value of an item, a verbal appraisal may be sufficient. Bear in mind that a verbal appraisal is just that—an opinion given only by word of mouth.

Written If an instrument is to be insured, a written appraisal will be necessary. A written appraisal is a signed document, desirable (and often required) for evaluation, and sometimes attribution of your instrument or bow. The value assigned in this case reflects the amount of money that would be required to replace it with a similar piece. Contemporary instruments and bows, if presented to the appraiser in good condition, are often the easiest to evaluate for replacement cost. The most common and accepted procedure is for the appraiser to contact the maker and determine what he or she would charge for a new work of similar quality—hence the term "replacement cost."

FEES

Ask up front what the cost of the appraisal will be. An appraisal, whether written or verbal, is a service performed for you by an expert. Prices vary according to the region and how competitive the market is. Simple insurance appraisals are the easiest to prepare, while estate and other legal appraisals constitute a greater amount of time and research. The charge should be a flat fee based on the hours spent, in accordance with IRS requirements that charges should not be based on a percentage of the assessed value.

THE APPRAISAL PROCESS

Establishing Authenticity Before a true appraisal can be given, questions of authenticity must be resolved. These issues are answered with widely accepted accompanying certificates, past appraisals, letters of provenance, and the appraiser's own expertise. If attribution is not an issue, the appraiser consults recent market data on similar pieces sold both privately and at auction. By talking to other dealers, reviewing sales results, and relying on their own experiences, appraisers can ascertain the replacement price of a given maker's work in similar style and condition.

Assessing Condition The greater the amount of previous repair work, no matter how well executed, the less value the instrument will have compared to an example in excellent condition.

Evaluating Cost Insurance appraisals are sometimes written ten to 15 percent higher than fair market value. Most insurers are comfortable with giving the client that extra cushion of protection, as they are paying for it in premium costs. They are not, however, comfortable with an item being overinsured. Appraisals written for estate or charitable-donation purposes are subject to stricter guidelines and regulations by both the courts and the IRS. They can be more complicated than other types of appraisals, requiring documented information as well as verification of the appraiser's qualifications and impartiality.

There are two important criteria for these types of appraisals: The first is the objectivity of the appraiser. The second is that the item be calculated according to the Fair Market Value scheme as defined by the IRS. For estate and charitable donations, all appraisals must be based on comparable sales results to support the evaluation. This means that the appraiser must have compiled a list of prices realized for similar or comparable instruments that have been sold in various markets, and be able to produce it on demand if your appraisal is ever called into question.

THE FINAL ASSESSMENT

The finished appraisal should be clear and concise. It should contain a full description of the instrument and its condition, detailing any major repair work, and it should be accompanied by a signed affidavit indicating when the piece was viewed, by whom it was evaluated, and which method of valuation (insurance value, fair-market value, and so on) was used.

A version of this chapter originally appeared in the June/July 2004 issue of Strings *magazine.*

CHAPTER 3

It's Valuation Day

Bringing your instrument to an auction specialist

BY ERIN SHRADER

You see one in the newspaper from time to time: a small ad placed by one of the auction houses announcing that its specialist will be visiting your city, offering a free and confidential valuation of your musical instruments. Just call for an appointment.

So I did call, mostly out of curiosity. I bought my violin from a friend purely for its sound, but dealers have always eyed it with curiosity, each offering a different idea about what it might be. Only one recalls having seen another like it and that instrument carried no label. Why not seek one more expert opinion?

One recent sunny afternoon I found myself on the third floor of a San Francisco building so discreet I nearly missed it, facing a plain wooden door simply marked "Sotheby's, Est. 1744. Please knock." The date alone is intimidating, never mind the reputation. Add 260 years of trading the world's most exclusive property—imagine knocking on that door with an ordinary violin.

Inside Paul Hayday was viewing instruments at a conference table in a small, warmly lit room lined with books. Eavesdropping on his earlier appointment, I was relieved to find that I was not the only person visiting out of simple curiosity.

Hayday turned out to be an engaging and knowledgeable young man who cheerfully gave his full attention to my 19th-century German violin. He turned it over and over, inspecting, measuring, and peering inside with a tiny light on a flexible wand. Even an ordinary violin can present a puzzle. The purfling on the top is quite different from the back, and the varnish on the scroll doesn't match the body. "Well, it's one thing to purfle a top and another to purfle a back," he pointed out, referring to the difference in hardness of spruce and maple. Either the varnish has been altered or the scroll may not belong, hard to say for sure.

Still, who has ever seen a violin by Otto Jager? Consulting his printout of violin auction results, he raised an eyebrow. None has ever sold at auction, which is highly unusual. My violin, while not valuable, is actually quite rare.

"He didn't make many," Hayday concluded.

Specialists from auction houses travel constantly in search of the instruments that fill their catalogs. He says a day rarely goes by that he doesn't see something interesting—as in valuable.

Many lots are consigned by dealers, organizations, or collectors. Still, unknown instruments are, indeed, discovered in the closets of the unsuspecting who have no idea what "grandpa" left them. These valuation events can be the first point of contact with the auction house for such families. Hayday has seen some of these instruments before and will see them again, establishing a relationship with the owners as they decide what to do with their property.

Not everyone makes an appointment with an eye toward selling. Some are actually interested in buying. Sotheby's keeps lists of clients and the kind of properties they are looking for. The man before me had an unusual instrument to be identified, which looked like a tiny double bass the size of a child's cello, and he was interested in buying other early music instruments.

While a specialist may give auction estimates, one of these brief visits is not an insurance appraisal, a conclusive valuation, or a positive identification. It may, however, be an opportunity to find out if you should seek further advice, or consider selling.

As for the value of my little-known violin? I forgot to ask! But I have no intention of selling.

A version of this chapter originally appeared in the June/July 2005 issue of Strings *magazine.*

CHAPTER 4

Do I Hear a Second?

Getting a second opinion is harder than you'd think

BY JAMES N. McKEAN

Before you buy an old house, you have it inspected. Before you buy a used car, you have your mechanic check it out. Before you buy an antique violin, you . . . swallow hard? Remind yourself that trust is the basis of all relationships?

You're about to lay out a sizable chunk of hard cash—perhaps an amount somewhere between the car and the house purchases—so it's only natural that you'd like some reassurance that what you're buying is what the dealer says it is and that it's not going to fall to pieces sometime down the road.

But what can you do? In all the talk about the sound and the maker and the market and how much your immensely talented child needs this instrument to proceed on the path to stardom and artistic expression, no one has said anything about those things that make you sit bolt upright at three in the morning.

Water in the basement? Termites? That burning smell after only 500 miles? How do you know that the same kind of thing won't happen with your new antique violin?

You want someone to take a look at it *before* you write the check: a second opinion.

But before you get to that point, there is a lot of work to be done. Don't worry, though: it all rests with the person showing you the violin or the bow.

No matter what stage you've reached in what can be a long and grueling process, keep this in mind: you're the one with the money. There are a lot more violins in the world than there are customers to buy them. It's the dealer's responsibility to provide you with all the available information on the instruments and bows he's offering, and that means both condition and authenticity. Without those assurances, don't take the violin out of the shop for trial.

In fact, don't even make an appointment to see it in the first place.

THE GUESSING GAME

I recently got a call from parents who have a daughter in the prep division of a prestigious conservatory. The time had come to step up to a full-size violin, and she had enough promise to warrant looking at a serious instrument. They had located a Chanot. It was being offered by a Midwest dealer for $48,000, and they wanted to know if this was a fair price. They also wanted me to take a look at the violin and tell them if the condition was okay.

It only took a few questions to discover that the dealer hadn't done his homework. Which Chanot? I asked; there were at least a dozen of the family who made violins, in both France and England, and the quality varied considerably, which needless to say is reflected in the price they command. Georges, was the answer; at least that was what was on the label, but the dealer felt that it was really the work of his son, Georges Adolphe, considered a much lesser maker. That was his opinion, but they already knew that he was not an authority in the field.

What kind of authentication did it have?

The dealer was being rather vague about that: the violin had some kind of papers, but he wasn't sure exactly what. He would ask the owners, if in the end they were serious about the violin.

Labels are easily and often forged, switched, and altered. It takes a true expert to know what a violin or bow really is. Unfortunately, there are very few experts, living or dead, so the provenance— the accumulated documentation—is critically important. Certificates, bills of sale, old insurance appraisals, articles in magazines, letters from previous owners, all these documents paint a picture of what the violin or bow has been represented to be in the past.

Be brave, be brazen; dealers love to talk about each other.

If certificates are provided, make sure they go with the violin or bow. Early certificates didn't have photographs; make sure the description and measurements match. If there are photographs, examine them closely, and make sure they match what is being offered. If the seller is only providing his or her own certification, then ask around: is it enough that you could resell the instrument based solely on that?

Use your teacher's contacts, if this is your first real violin, to find out more about the seller with whom you are dealing. He or she can always give you the name of someone to ask, and that person can give you another, and so on.

Be brave, be brazen. Dealers love to talk about each other. They're in competition (except when they're working together, which you wouldn't know), so you can expect a certain amount of trash talking, but after a while a picture will begin to emerge.

Confirming authenticity is only half the problem. The other half is condition. Again, you might want an independent evaluation. But before you go in search of one, the dealer should provide you with a written report that details the condition of the instrument: the varnish, the major repairs, the originality of each part (top, back, ribs, and scroll).

Most importantly, the report must be accompanied by a schematic drawing that shows every single instance of damage or repair.

Beyond that, ultraviolet and infrared photography will reveal retouching, a clue to damage and repairs. A CAT scan can show worm damage and hidden cracks. For bows, an x-ray will show any damage to the head, which is important because a broken head can be repaired invisibly with screws.

Dendrochronology (the measurement of the growth rings in the top) can help date the violin, but it's very expensive, so it doesn't make sense except with instruments at the top end of the market.

GET IT IN WRITING

The written condition report is what you'll get with most instruments. With it, though, you should also ask for what kind of assurances you can expect as to any repairs that have been done. Violins are under constant stress, so no one can guarantee that any repair will hold forever, but a reputable shop will stand behind the condition of what it sells, so that you won't be stuck with the bill if something does open up.

If you do buy the violin, ask for any guarantees in writing. There has been a tremendous proliferation of non-violin makers dealing fiddles in recent years.

That can be a real problem when it comes to repairs, let alone routine maintenance. Who will do it? And if the dealer has no bench experience, who is writing the condition report? It takes a skilled restorer to do a detailed evaluation.

Once you have all the proper documentation, ask for copies to take with the violin for trial. Be up front—tell the dealer that you intend to get a second opinion.

"We have no problem with people asking for a second opinion," says Chris Reuning, a prominent violin maker and dealer in Boston. "If you're dealing with a legitimate firm, the most important factor is whether it stands behind what it sells. I feel that it's a professional responsibility to my clients to offer them advice, including questions about authenticity, condition, and value. But show the condition report with the violin. And there should be nothing secretive about it— the minute it becomes that, it brings into question whether it's a professional opinion."

Before you take the instrument out on approval, ask what kind of insurance covers the violin. It has nothing to do with a second opinion, but it's of vital importance to be absolutely clear about what liability you might incur if something were to happen to the instrument or bow while it's in your possession. Not just whether it's insured, but whether you are also covered under the policy. Every dealer has insurance to cover the instrument in case of damage or loss; not all have a policy that covers you, the person trying it out.

Again, make sure you have it in writing: it should be part of the sign-out form.

NOW YOU'RE READY

At last, it's time for a second opinion. But this is where you hit the brick wall. No independent violin maker or restorer that I know will give one. Why not? The fear of litigation. Carla Shapreau, who co-authored the book *Violin Fraud: Deception, Forgery, and Lawsuits in England and America* (Oxford University Press, 1997), covers the liabilities a shop might face in some detail.

"Even if you did all the right things and engaged in reasonable conduct as an expert, this would not prevent someone from suing you," she says. "At the end of the day even if you were victorious you might have to shell out high attorney's fees and court costs. And a claim like this could arise decades after an opinion is given."

This is not theoretical. Everyone in the business is well aware that one of our colleagues a few years ago was forced to buy a Gagliano violin that he had checked over, but missed an acoustic patch on the inside of the back. It wasn't at all certain that it affected the value of the violin, but just the cost of litigation would have been ruinous, so he had no choice but to buy the violin.

Any restorer has to ask himself, why take the risk? Particularly when it's someone buying a violin from someone else.

There are some intermediaries who, seeing the need, have begun offering their services to broker the transaction—for a fee, of course. Stay as far away from them as you can. It's a very, very small business, and you can't be sure that the person you've hired is working just for you.

As enticing as the idea of a second opinion might be, in the end the only thing that matters is the shop you're buying the violin from. There's no way around the fact that antique violins are a risky business.

All you can do is minimize the risk, and the best way to do that is to limit your search to legitimate dealers, and then get the assurances you need from the shop you're dealing with.

A version of this chapter originally appeared in the June/July 2006 issue of Strings *magazine.*

CHAPTER 5

Sticker Shock

Labels aren't always what they seem

⌒

BY JAMES N. McKEAN

G o into a store and buy a box of Kleenex or even a Ferrari (hey, might as well dream, right?) and you may have a lot of questions about what you've just acquired. In the case of the Ferrari, you'll probably suffer buyer's remorse, but the last thing you will ever question is whether you bought the real thing. In the world of violins, however, the rules are quite a bit different. While it's true that the label is more often than not correct—outright fraud is not that common—that does not mean that the violin is what the label says it is.

The most frequent call that any violin maker or instrument dealer gets is not someone looking for an instrument or bow. It is from someone who has opened an old violin case—usually it was granddad's, brought from Europe—and found, inside the f-hole, a faded label that reads Stradivari, Guarneri, Amati, or Stainer.

And with it, a bow stamped Tourte.

Well, don't put a down payment on that condo in Boca quite yet—99.9 percent of the time, these items are inexpensive trade instruments and bows. Fraud? No. The label was never intended to make you think it was the real thing. Rather, it was put in to indicate the model used in the copying process. If you look very closely inside that assumed Italian instrument, in tiny script, it just might say, "Made in Germany." And yet hope springs eternal; I had one caller ask if Stradivari might have had a summer house in Germany.

Sure, every violin is worth something; but almost always these instruments are not worth much more than it would take to put them in playing condition.

The fiddle trade runs on romance. Famous violins have names and pedigrees, sometimes picaresque enough to make the Red Violin pale by comparison. It's worth remembering, though, that a romance is not much fun without a good villain or two. It should come as no surprise that labels have been faked in an outright attempt to deceive. After all, the same violin might sell for ten times what it would otherwise if attributed to a known maker or a better one.

The situation is further complicated by the fact that many stringed instruments, even those of the most celebrated masters, left the shop unlabelled. Unfortunately, no one bothered to tell those luthiers that they weren't making musical instruments, they were making future priceless antiques.

Still, one of the two fundamental things that apply to the fiddle trade is that it's almost impossible to sell a fiddle without some kind of label in it. So the label in your violin most likely is correct. And if it isn't, don't jump to the sad conclusion that it's just one more example of human greed; it's probably just somebody's best guess as to what it is.

To help navigate the often confusing maze of stringed-instrument labels, there's a plethora of dictionaries of violin makers, some with extensive compilations of reproductions of labels. Keep in mind, though, that the label might just be a reproduction and that it takes a trained eye to tell the difference. Here are a few reliable sources:

The New Encyclopedia of Violin and Bow Makers by Andreas Preuss (Andreas Preuss, www.andreaspreuss.com, $60). In this recent compilation, Preuss has weeded out the myths and tales that make older dictionaries fun to read but suspect as reference works. Available on CD-ROM only, but that makes it easy for the database to be frequently updated.

Dictionnaire Universel des Luthiers by Rene Vannes and Claude Lebet (Les Amis de la Musique, Brussels). This is an excellent source, and since the working vocabulary you need is so small (varnish=vernis, and so on) you don't even need to know French to seem worldly and erudite.

The Violin Makers of the United States by Thomas James Wenberg (Pizzicato Pub Co, October 1986). Sadly out of print, but worth searching out.

Ungarischer Geigenbau (The Violin Makers of Hungary) by Peter Benedek (a catalog of a 1995 exhibition of violins presented at the Stadtmuseum in Munich; in German and English, 1997, €200). A most reliable source for a part of the violin world that is rife with mistaken identity, some of it even unintentional.

Encyclopedia of Violin-Makers by Karel Jalovec. (Paul Hamlyn, Ltd., London/ England, 1968). Another out-of-print book, but a good resource for looking up labels.

A version of this chapter originally appeared in the July 2003 issue of Strings *magazine.*

CHAPTER 6

Going Once, Going Twice

Shopping the violin auctions—a primer for musicians

BY ERIN SHRADER

Long tables, crowded with double rows of violins and violas in various states of repair, fill the preview gallery at Skinner auction house in Boston. A few resemble carcasses, with big cracks or missing pieces. Others are in perfect playing condition. Most fall somewhere in between. A couple of ratty old bows serve those who simply must play something in order to make a decision. It's easy to pick the dealers out from the throng. Moving methodically down the rows, catalogs in hand, they dispassionately examine each lot, making notes on condition and how much they might be willing to spend.

No need to play, they know by looking, and there are 400 lots to get through, not to mention another 500 across the street at Tarisio, or the 200 they saw a few days ago at Christie's in New York.

A teenager with a head of curls, a short plaid skirt, and proud stage parents is also making her way through the tables, bow in hand, playing anything with strings on it. No quick trial notes for her, she performs entire pieces on each instrument. Behind their catalogs the dealers roll their eyes. Across the street at the

Tarisio preview, a teacher is vetting the sale for his students, while across the room a little boy is tearing through Paganini on one of the offered instruments. Barely more than elbow height to the grownups, he plays with alarming precision and musicality, and only on the very finest instruments. He garners a bit less eye-rolling from the dealers.

These are the faces of a slow-growing, but persistent trend. Once regarded as the exclusive turf of the professional dealer, the auction market is seeing musicians enter in greater numbers, and at all levels, from families looking for a good step-up value to famous soloists spending hundreds of thousands of dollars for prize Italian cellos, and patrons willing to drop millions on a Strad. They're drawn by the hope of a good deal, a huge selection of instruments, and a transparent marketplace with no hype, no salesman.

But there is pressure—several people will want the same instrument, there is no price tag, and auctions are fast-paced. If you bid in person, you will have seconds to decide how badly you want this instrument. Will you bid higher or let it go? Blink and it's gone. And remember, everything is sold as is. While the staff at the auction house has no reason to hide anything and will always disclose condition to the best of their knowledge, no one is going to take the item back if problems turn up later. Still, it's a challenge musicians are increasingly willing to take, especially in the United States, according to Christie's musical instrument specialist Kerry Keane, who works on both sides of the Atlantic. "That's cultural," he says, "Americans are more willing to take the bull by the horns."

Faced with hundreds of instruments, catalogs full of unfamiliar language, and a room full of cool, seasoned professionals, how does one approach said bull?

WHERE TO BEGIN

As a preliminary step to any serious shopping, Eric Merrill, who repairs instruments at Reuning and Son in Boston, suggests educating yourself by spending time in violin shops. It's a good way to develop a frame of reference for what is available, how much it costs, and to gain a sense of good quality, set up, and condition. Merrill cautions against the temptation of online auctions that don't specialize in violins. Having tried that game, Merrill always found "more wrong with it than I expected."

Only three companies hold musical-instrument auctions in the United States. Christie's in New York and Skinner in Boston are traditional auction houses with musical instrument departments headed by an expert, called the "specialist." They hold two sales a year, spring and fall, with public previews followed by a live sale.

Tarisio, a relative newcomer, is an Internet auction company, selling only bowed instruments and such related items as supplies, books, and memorabilia. Like the traditional houses, Tarisio produces a catalog and holds public previews, setting up in New York and Boston, attracting the crowd from the Christie's and Skinner viewings. But the sale is conducted later over the Internet.

"I thought there was a lot of potential in the auction business," says Chris Reuning, longtime dealer and founding partner in Tarisio. Reuning watched the development of eBay with interest, thinking the Internet suited violin auctions, especially for 'musicians. The pace is slower, and bidding from the familiar comfort of home is less intimidating than the atmosphere of the sale room. Dealers grumbled that they didn't have time to monitor the computer and bid as each item came up. But, building on their existing reputations as dealers, Ruening and partners Dmitry Gindin and Jason Price hoped to court the musicians directly.

Each auction house website contains information on buying, selling, and getting a copy of the catalog. All three houses sell a printed catalog and offer viewing online. Read the fine print carefully if you decide to buy or sell, as these details explicitly define the terms of the sale. The precise meaning of words used to describe instruments, how payment is received, and the amount of the auction house commissions vary by company.

DECIPHERING THE CATALOG

The catalog lists every lot in the sale, with some sort of description. A "lot" can contain one or several items sold together for one price. The terse descriptions that accompany each lot are a sort of short-hand, packing much information in a small space. Details such as measurements are fairly straightforward; the following terms require further explanation.

The last item listed is an estimated price range. Reuning puts it simply: the low estimate is what he figures a dealer would pay and high estimate is closer to retail. When a dealer shops at auction, he figures what he can sell the instrument for, subtracts the cost of repairs (he probably has violin makers in his employ), and decides how much he can afford to pay. Behind the low estimate is a confidential "reserve," the price below which the item won't be sold, to protect the seller. Estimates are on the low side, as buyers love the perception of a bargain and won't be inclined to consider anything overpriced. Because the buyers at auction are generally well-informed, the closing price tends to be fair-market value.

David Bonsey, specialist at Skinner, defines fair-market value as what an informed buyer will pay for a particular piece in cash. Fair-market value, he says, is

Once regarded as the exclusive turf of the professional dealer, the auction market is seeing musicians enter in greater numbers.

specific to each piece, and is determined by a combination of attribution (who made it), the quality of the work, and its present condition. These factors are hinted at in the catalog language describing each lot.

When a maker's name appears without qualification, for example, "Antonio Stradivari," the attribution is certain. In the case of very important instruments, it's backed up by the consensus of experts. Short of a definitive attribution, qualifiers such as "attributed to," may appear, reflecting the level of uncertainty. Details vary, but in general "attributed to" means probably by the person named, but there is some reasonable doubt, while "ascribed to" is a little less certain. "Labeled" implies that the instrument is probably *not* by that maker, although it is labeled or brand-stamped as such.

As Keane tells clients at Christie's, "Labels are as changeable as a pair of shoes."

Quality refers to quality of sound and workmanship, but also quality in relation to the maker's other work. (Is this the maker's best work? Nice looking but so-so sounding?) Tarisio's catalog uses terms such as "fine" or "good" to denote better-quality materials and workmanship.

Condition reports may include any damage, old repairs, wear and tear, deformed ribs or arches, "worm" damage, the condition of the varnish, and whether all parts are original. A condition report is available on all instruments and bows, written by the specialist, to the best of his ability, as a service to the buyer. Always request a condition report for any lot you're seriously considering, and examine the instrument yourself. Ask any questions that arise; the auction house has nothing to hide.

Two additional factors, provenance and freshness, can come into play, particularly in the nose-bleed price ranges. Who owned it, who played it, association with historical events, or even good stories attached to the instrument all contribute to provenance. Freshness to the market is more ephemeral. As Keane explains, when an instrument has been off the market for a long time, it generates interest, a perception of discovery.

DO YOUR HOMEWORK

The selection at auction is truly overwhelming, so go through the catalog or website ahead of time to get an idea of what you're looking for—old, modern, French, a viola of a certain size, or simply the best violin or cello you can get at the price you can afford.

If you've settled on an instrument, do your homework, says Reuning, especially if you're considering a big purchase—say, a Balestrieri. Find out what the maker's instruments have sold for recently. Call around to dealers and see what they're asking. Check *The Red Book*, an auction price guide published annually by Donald M. Cohen. This book also contains handy appendices on historical style points, brand stamps, and even fictitious names of violin and bow makers. A record of past auction results is available online at Tarisio and from other sources.

Call the specialist in charge to discuss authenticity, if attribution is an important factor in the price. Read the fine print, cautions Reuning. That overrides the specialist's word in case of dispute. Tarisio offers a 20-day guarantee of authenticity on instruments it definitively identifies as by the maker named. Reuning advises agreeing in advance whose expert opinion both parties will accept in case of a dispute.

Get the condition report. Finding someone to offer advice on condition is not a bad idea, especially if you don't feel knowledgeable enough to make an informed decision. If possible, find a disinterested, but knowledgeable party, such as a repairer or maker you know and trust. Dealers are knowledgeable, but not unbiased—they buy at auction, too. A handful of luthiers do make themselves available for a very reasonable fee, and the specialist may be able to make a referral.

Decide ahead of time what your selection is worth and what you can spend. Keep in mind that the hammer price is only part of the total financial picture. On top of that is the Buyer's Premium, anywhere from 15 to 20 percent of the hammer price; taxes, if applicable; shipping and insurance charges if you will not be collecting the instrument in person; any necessary repairs; and travel expenses if you are from out of the area. Subtract these from the total you can spend to figure the hammer price you can afford.

All this footwork is, in short, what a dealer does for an instrument offered in his shop, and is accounted for in the retail markup.

Historically, auction prices have been wholesale, about half of retail, so by doing the homework behind a wise purchase, you may well be able to find a good deal.

As Merrill, the violin repairman, says, "Time or money, you're going to spend one or the other."

THE PREVIEW

Seeing and trying an instrument are vitally important to a player. Bonsey of Skinner recommends scheduling a private preview time. "All you have to do is call," he confirms. "There's no quicker way to learn." Even if you don't find your instrument

Always request a condition report for any lot you're seriously considering.

today, seeing and trying many instruments is part of your education as a string player.

Ask the specialists for suggestions, or ask questions about instruments you've picked out of the lineup. They've catalogued every instrument in the room. When families come in to Christie's, Keane says he always takes out the catalog and circles the good-quality instruments in their price range, steering them away from instruments with condition issues. If you happen to fall in love with something that needs work, keep in mind the cost of repairs and the difficulty of finding someone to do the work in some parts of the country. Ask around: musicians will know if this is a problem in your area.

Of the instruments and bows in good condition in your price range, simply choose the ones that sound best to you. Have someone else play it for you, but don't be swayed by someone else's opinion. "Trust your instinct," advises Bonsey. "You can tell after the first few minutes if it's right for you."

BIDDING

Once you've chosen a fiddle or two, or three, there are several ways to bid. Regardless of the method, all bidders register with the auction house, which will require some form of identification and possibly financial information to ensure ability to pay. For example, at Skinner, Bonsey explains, "If the interest is in an expensive lot, the bidder may be asked for bank information or information on a line of credit that will cover the amount he or she intends to bid." Also, each company accepts different means of payment, so call ahead with questions on financial matters.

If you can't or would prefer not to attend a live sale, you can leave an absentee bid with the auction house. You can do this in person, by phone, fax, mail, or email, depending on the house. When your item comes up, the auctioneer will "execute" your bid incrementally, as you would in person, up to your maximum. You may get it for less, but you won't be tempted to go higher. You can also call in to cancel a bid.

If you cannot attend but wish to bid "live," arrange for a phone line. Someone from the auction house will call you a few minutes before your lot comes up, preferably on a land line rather than a cell phone, and will bid for you from the side of the sales room. Skinner offers yet another option: an online link to Live Auctioneers enables bidding in real time at live auctions around the world via the Internet.

Decisions must be made in seconds. It's easy to get attached to a certain lot and bid more than your maximum. For that reason, Reuning, whose company Tarisio does not hold a live sale at all, advises leaving a bid or getting a phone line as protection against getting caught up in the drama in the room, and as a way to keep your business confidential.

Reuning maintains that Tarisio's Internet format is more comfortable for musicians. The pace is slower and no one knows who is bidding, since everyone uses a made-up bidder ID.

The format also offers another advantage for private bidders. "The Internet gets rid of the monkey business in the back of the auction room." By this Reuning means the practice of "ringing" an item, in which two dealers who want the same lot will agree to buy it together rather than competing with each other, thereby suppressing the price. They can share in the profit later. This agreement can happen on the spot, with a wink or a nod. This might happen in the case of a "sleeper"—something desirable that has been missed by the auction specialist, or assigned a very low estimate for some other reason.

Bonsey, at Skinner, says: "I think being in the room is still the best way."

If you decide to go live, get a paddle and find a seat. The front of the room affords the best view of the podium; from the back of the room you can watch the competition. The families are easy to pick out, the high-rollers are nearly impossible—they're probably on the phone.

The auctioneer doesn't use the lightning-fast patter of the old-time auctioneer, but lots do move by quickly. At Christie's, the reader board over her head helps viewers keep track of the action, with bids coming from the room, the phone, and the auctioneer, herself, who executes the absentee bids. The bidding starts low and moves up by pre-determined increments. For lots in the $500 to $1,000 range, the increment might be $50, while lots in the millions may move at $100,000 per bid. If the bidding pauses, but there is still interest, the auctioneer may cut the increment, prolonging the final sale.

The atmosphere can be dramatic, as prices spiral upward and hopeful bidders are forced to let go of a desired instrument, or a sullen-looking teenager sits bolt upright upon winning his prize cello then scoots out the back door to high-five his buddies with a great big grin.

As Keane says, "Auction is good theater and good theater is drama. And we create that from the podium."

A version of this chapter originally appeared in the October 2006 issue of Strings *magazine.*

CHAPTER 7

Cyberspace Shopping Tips

The Internet ushers in a brave new world

⌒

BY DAVID TEMPLETON

t's a brave new world. In times past, whenever a musician set off to acquire a fine old violin or cello, the course was fairly clear, leading either to a professional dealer with an established reputation, or to the auction house. Since the rise of the Internet, however, with countless violin sellers hanging out their virtual shingles—and the emergence of such online rummage sales as eBay and Yahoo—the violinless violinist can now go shopping for that instrument without ever leaving his or her home-office computer. While the wisdom of engaging in high-level Web commerce is still being debated, the Internet obviously has changed the way humans do business. The Net already has spawned one online auction house—Tarisio—devoted exclusively to stringed-instrument sales, and it's beginning to change the way a cellist goes about looking for a cello. Shocking, but true.

Here are a few good words of advice when buying instruments on the Internet to help safeguard your investment:

KNOW WHAT YOU'RE BUYING

"It is very important," counsels Philip Scott of Bonhams, "to ask about the condition of the instrument. Ask for details. The more specific your questioning, the more likely you are to get a good idea of what the instrument's condition really is." This means asking for a copy of the label (maker name, model, year made, and location where the instrument was crafted) as well as the instrument's measurements; requesting information on cracks, repairs, and blemishes; asking about the fittings; and finding out if the instrument comes with a bow and/or case. And be sure to inquire about the return policy; some (but not all) sellers will allow a short window of opportunity for the buyer to examine the instrument, but be aware that you might incur the shipping costs even if you choose not to keep the instrument.

SEE FOR YOURSELF

Says Tim Ingles of Sotheby's, "The golden rule—never buy a violin without seeing it—to check its authenticity, condition, and sound, applies even more so in the case of buying online." Reputable dealers will let you inspect the merchandise before the sale or auction, an opportunity you should always take before spending any significant amount of money. If you can't see it in person, ask for detailed photos.

KNOW YOUR PRICE

"Always know exactly what you are able to spend," says Tarisio's Jason Price. "In auctions, sometimes, you have people spending more than they want to or need to." Entrepeneur.com also recommends that you make sure that you and the seller can agree on the form of payment before the deal closes. Is the seller willing to accept a personal check? Are you willing to wait to receive your purchase until a check clears? Is credit-card payment available? Is the seller using a secure method of accepting credit cards like PayPal?

GET ADVICE

Says David Bonsey of Skinner, Inc., "For anyone buying at auction, Internet or otherwise, the most important thing is to know and trust your specialist. Any reputable auction house will have its own music-department specialist available to answer questions about the instruments to be auctioned."

A version of this chapter originally appeared in the July 2003 issue of Strings *magazine.*

CHAPTER 8

Heirloom or Junk?

The flea-market fiddle: Say, that's a good buy!
Or say goodbye to your cash?

BY STEPHEN K. PERRY

The flea market violin calls you over, lying in the old coffin case, ancient gut strings springing from the head, crackled brown varnish. "Grandpa's fiddle: $275." Buying a flea market or eBay fiddle is a bit like buying an unrestored vintage car—test drives rarely reveal the ultimate potential. Good commercial violins of the 19th and early 20th centuries are not uncommon. But rarely does a nice 18th-century master violin turn up. A nonexpert can avoid severe buyer's remorse by looking, listening, and feeling for indicators of quality and condition.

Unlike the staff at a good violin shop, the folks holding a yard sale are not likely to be violin experts. They may have a story about where the fiddle came from or who owned it, but when it comes to assessing its value and condition, you'll be pretty much on your own. Here are a few things to consider before making a purchase.

TAKE A GOOD LOOK

Does the violin look visually distinctive (usually the sign of a single maker), like a good piece of art? Most modern violins are smooth and sleek, following the Italian school. Others are square and clunky looking, not a good sign, but not terminal. Before beginning your search, take a look at the crisp and cohesive work of the great masters in violin books or old auction catalogs at your local library.

Make sure the violin for sale matches modern dimensional requirements. I use an inexpensive metric cloth tape from a sewing shop. A typical body length is 356 mm (just over 14 inches) measured on the back from the edge next to the button—the half round at the base of the neck—to the edge by the endpin. Anything less is likely to be a small-size student violin worth very little. The "stop" distance from the inner f-hole notch to the edge of the top by the neck should be close to 195 mm (just under $7\frac{3}{4}$ inches). The distance from the edge of the top to the intersection of the nut and fingerboard should be about 130 mm (a little over 5 inches). Serious deviations from these dimensions do not bode well.

The top and back should be gracefully shaped, with the channel—the dip just in from the edge—even and well carved, passing smoothly across the corners. The arching should flow smoothly up from the edge to the centerline. Bulbous or goat-backed arching indicates low-quality factory work.

Purfling, corners, and edgework are a builder's acid test. Sloppy or scratched-in purfling—look for wood grain going through the twin lines—suggests fast factory work, but excessive precision may indicate machine work. Poorly shaped corners stand out. For the typical Stradivari-style violin, the corners should flare a little towards the end, reaching into the C-bout.

The f-holes should also be a good visual match to the overall style—they should be cleanly cut, showing skilled knife work. The edges of the f-holes also reveal the thickness of the top. Anything over 3 mm is rather thick and likely the mark of a cheap factory fiddle.

Look for a smoothly cut scroll with flowing lines, careful undercutting, and a sense of liveness rather than a static appearance (the instrument shouldn't look clunky or disconnected). Scrolls grafted onto new necks sometimes indicate old violins. A violin with a grafted neck indicates better factory work and may be an old instrument.

Look along the fingerboard for distortion and warping. The fingerboard should have a slight scoop of about 1 mm to allow the strings to vibrate freely. If the violin has strings, then simply pressing one down by the nut and at the end of the fingerboard will show a gap under the center. This gap is the amount of scoop. The fingerboard should be about 4 mm thick at the end and about 5 mm thick along the sides of the neck. A thin, warped, or humped fingerboard may require expensive replacement. The highest part of the end of the fingerboard should be about 21 mm above the top. Much lower and the neck may need an expensive reset.

Pegbox cracks are bad news, as are poorly fitting, irregularly turning pegs. If the shafts are large in diameter or the heads are right up against the pegbox wall, the violin needs pegwork. This can be expensive if the holes are worn and require bushing, where a plug of boxwood or spiral of maple is used to fill the old hole and a new hole is reamed.

The interior reveals even more about the violin. Insert a dentist's mirror through an f-hole or peek through the endpin hole to see whether the top was roughly cut out or smoothly carved. See whether the bass bar was hacked out of the same wood as the top or fitted and shaped, or whether it shows serious repair work. A smooth top interior and smoothly shaped, glued-in bass bar are signs of good workmanship. The linings reinforcing the ribs at their contact with the top and back should lie cleanly against the ribs and be nicely shaped, as should the blocks reinforcing the corners. Some inexpensive violins do not have blocks in the corners.

Well-known commercial labels of student-level violins are most likely accurate. But maker's labels are more problematic and should not be trusted without expert verification.

Cheap varnish generally chips easily rather than wearing gracefully, and often shows white powder where scratched. Hard thick varnish can stifle a violin. Many violins have poorly applied varnish over the original, but sometimes a gem lurks under the polyurethane.

Varnish color on good violins is usually elegant and softer than the garish colors created by excessive amounts of chemical dyes. Nevertheless, good-playing violins sometimes show up in dark, muddy, or lurid varnish. Regardless, a totally smooth high-gloss shine is not typical of very good violins.

LISTEN INTENTLY

Most violinists can tell the potential of a strung violin, even with dead strings, but even an unstrung violin can be heard. Tap the body gently around the edges of the top and back. The tapped pitch of the top and back tells much about the thickness of the plates. A very thick top produces a higher, short-lasting pitch, while a thinner top produces a lower pitch and rings nicely. Tapping all over the top and back can show the regularity of thickness. Thicker spots produce a hard, thudding sound. A good violin's plates usually ring nicely and show no sudden changes in thickness.

If the violin has strings on it, pluck each one and listen to the character of tone, and whether the volume or pitch wavers. Ideally each string will produce a clear, steady tone of roughly the same volume as the other strings. Bowing even dead strings evaluates string-to-string balance, variations in violin response up and down each string—and the overall response of the violin, to some extent. A dead string is dead all the way up and down. New strings won't fix a hole in the response.

Active violin hunters would do well to carry with them the aforementioned dentist's mirror, plus a set of strings, a tuning fork, and a self-fitting bridge (a self-adjusting bridge with pivoting feet; to install you simply press the bridge down on the belly of the instrument and the feet will adjust on their own). Listen for buzzes and unusual vibrations. If the source isn't apparent, keep in mind the potential cost of finding and repairing these problems.

FEEL CAREFULLY

Violinists have sensitive touch—a great help in evaluating a violin. Try playing the violin with closed eyes and pay close attention to the neck. A thick and clubby neck is the mark of an inferior violin. (I've never picked up a good fiddle built with a clunky neck—one of the easier things to evaluate. A perfect neck always makes me look very carefully at the rest of the fiddle!) At the same time, the fingertips can search out humps and dips in the fingerboard that may require a luthier's attention. Carefully press the top towards the center of each f-hole very lightly, but only if there are no cracks. The top should have a slight amount of spring. Finally, feel the weight of the violin and how it rides in playing position. A good violin feels light and comfortable under the chin and lets the left hand shift smoothly.

CHOOSE WISELY

Go for the good stuff, leave the rest—and don't pay too much! Careful appreciation of a mystery violin using all the senses gives many clues to quality. A little study and practice will help you interpret these clues.

Happy hunting!

A version of this chapter originally appeared in the April 2004 issue of Strings *magazine.*

CHAPTER 9

Market Report

Should you buy overseas?

BY MARY VAN CLAY

A ny musician traveling overseas is likely to be tantalized by more than just the music, food, and culture of another country. It's hard not to hanker after the instruments, which often somehow seem more mysterious, romantic, and better-sounding than those you already have. But is this, in the midst of your travels, a good time and place to shop for another instrument or bow? Purchasing this way can be a good idea, but it's not a venture to be taken lightly. You could end up paying a high price for the romance of Italian or Parisian provenance without getting the quality you could find more easily right at home.

Europe is a particularly seductive destination for the string player. Cremona, in the Lombardy region of Italy, is perhaps the most famous site for violin making in the world, since it was there, in the 16th century, that the Amati family raised the craft to an art. With its native sons including both Antonio Stradivari and the Guarneris, the city has been renowned ever since. Today it still boasts more than 100 professional violin and bow makers, the Scuola Internazionale di Liuteria (the International Violin Making School), and a triennial instrument-making competition.

Dozens of other European cities can lay claim to one or more famous makers, and several entire towns are known for the craft. France's Mirecourt, in Lorraine, was famous from about 1840 to 1930 for good instruments of the type that would be called "student" violins today (and many fine individual makers got their start there). The town is no longer as central to the trade today. In southeastern Germany, Markneukirchen was a center for violin making until the end of World War II, and Bubenreuth is still a thriving center for good student instruments, though most of these are sold (often exported) through larger companies, not by individual makers.

Naturally, cosmopolitan centers such as London and Paris, which have always attracted music students and concertizers, also boast many dealers' shops and individual makers. London is also home to the well-known auction houses Bonhams, Christie's, Phillips, and Sotheby's, which all have important musical instrument divisions specializing in the violin family. Modern communication and delivery services, however, mean that the entire industry is much more decentralized today. Makers set up shops in every nook and cranny of the globe, and often attend one or more international trade events. Perhaps the most accessible to players is Musicora, the annual music trade show held in Paris every April. Violin makers come from down the street and across time zones to exhibit their wares, providing players with a terrific opportunity to try out instruments in a relatively pressure-free environment. MusikMesse in Frankfurt provides a similar opportunity, although this exhibition is geared more toward the trade than toward individual consumers.

Exciting as it may seem to combine violin shopping with café-hopping, however, the American buyer should note that the supposed romance of a foreign label is not a sufficient basis for an instrument purchase. "There are a lot of [instruments] being passed off as great that are actually junk. You're paying a lot simply because you got it in, say, Italy—that's the romance factor," says Ralph Rabin, a maker and dealer in Madison, Wisconsin, who frequently imports instruments during his visits to Cremona and other European cities. Indeed, players are increasingly wise to the fact that a contemporary violin made in Italy is not intrinsically better than one made in Finland, New York, California, or Hong Kong.

The best reason to buy overseas is because a specific maker whose works you admire happens to live there. Cellist Hai-Ye Ni, who was in Italy and stopped in Cremona to look at instruments, was drawn not by the city's history but by resident luthier Francesco Bissolotti. "I'd heard good things about him from a friend," she says.

Another reason not to buy overseas without sufficient motivation is that it's simply more difficult, especially if you're dealing with a different language and set of shopping assumptions. Rabin says, "Let's say you go into any given shop, with X amount to spend," he says. "You'll want to see a variety in that price range. In England and Germany, shops are similar to the States, where you'd go into a shop and have several makers, old and new, represented. And it's quite easy in Paris on the rue de Rome, because all the violin shops are together. So it facilitates the process—but remember, you'll be paying Parisian prices as well! It is expensive to run those [shops].

"And in Italy, it's every maker for himself. So you'd have to have a really good memory of sound, because you're probably not going to be allowed to take one instrument across the street to another shop to make a comparison. And you're probably not going to be allowed to take it out on loan; they don't know who you are."

Then there's the question of follow-up service. "That was one of the things that prevented me from saying I wanted to buy [Bissolotti's] cello right then," says the New York-based Ni. "A new instrument changes so much the first year. I'd like to have the convenience of just riding on the train for half an hour to take it to the maker so he could take a look at it and adjust it." By contrast, if you buy a foreign-made instrument from a local business, like Rabin's, that shop will take on the task of providing you with adjustments and other services.

Then you need to consider the ups and downs of your purchasing power—is the exchange rate favorable?—and sales and importation costs. In many European countries, for example, you will have to pay a Value Added Tax (VAT) at the time of purchase; although this amount (17.5 percent in the U.K.) is refunded to nonresidents, you will have to go through paperwork and perhaps a waiting period before getting your money back. And of course you will need to pay a customs duty, based on the total value of your instrument, upon reentry into the U.S. If you ship the instrument or bow instead of carrying it home with you, not only are you paying for that service, but your personal customs exemption for a portion of item's cost (usually the first $400) is lost.

Finally, shipping your goods home is an important consideration. "Even with well padded cases, I've still had a violin neck break," says Rabin. "And you're at risk if you don't have [the new purchase] insured [for overseas travel]. You're more likely to be insured for things you buy here, under a homeowner's or professional policy."

All this is not to say musicians shouldn't buy instruments overseas. Today's communication methods create exciting opportunities for the American instrument buyer. Cellist Hai-Ye Ni, for instance, is looking forward to revisiting Bissolotti's shop when she returns to Italy, and she may decide to go ahead and purchase, now that she's had time to shop around and make mental comparisons. But, as she herself says, a buyer should not fall simply for the romance of a European label.

A version of this chapter originally appeared in the April 1998 issue of Strings *magazine.*

CHAPTER 10

Got Coverage?

The ins and outs of instrument insurance

BY ERIN SHRADER

D isaster happens in an eye blink. A violinist drops a fine French bow, snapping the head off. It's repairable, but now worth a fraction of its former value. Someone bumps into a fiddler putting on a shoulder rest before a gig and sends his only violin clattering to the floor, breaking the neck out of the body.

While money can't undo the damage, it can make life less painful in the aftermath. Instruments and bows are notoriously fragile and expensive to repair or replace, so most string players should consider insuring their property. Adding coverage to an existing homeowner's or renter's policy can be an easy and economical route for some. Others will be best served by a musical-instrument policy placed directly with one of the handful of carriers specializing in insuring the music industry.

Insurance, with all its myriad details and arcane technical terms, can be confusing. Taking time to learn about the issues that are particular to covering musical instruments and assessing your needs will help you determine the best coverage for you. Read the fine print, ask questions, and compare policies to find the coverage best suited to your situation.

WHAT IT COVERS

Insurance protects your instruments against damage and loss due to accidents. According to Ellis Hershman of Heritage Insurance Services, a leading insurer of the music trades, breakage and the resulting loss of value are the most common claims filed by string players. Musical-instrument policies are set up to cover this "devaluation" and similar protection can be negotiated through your homeowner policy.

"Scheduled" items (insurance lingo for items listed on your policy) are insured for the replacement value, which is often, but not always, determined by appraisal. This protects the value of your investment from devaluation due to damage, which is particularly important for antique instruments and bows, whose value is based largely on condition. Say that aforementioned symphony player's bow was valued and insured at $15,000 in pure condition, but now worth only $1,500 as the result of the accident. With devaluation coverage, the insurance settlement would pay the price of repair plus the $13,500 loss of value.

Good coverage is "all-risk," meaning there are very few exclusions, or reasons that your incident would not be covered, and "worldwide," which means you are covered wherever you may be.

WHAT IT DOESN'T COVER

What insurance doesn't cover is spelled out in the exclusions. Wear and tear is not normally covered, nor is damage from mold, rust, rats, or other vermin. Read the fine print, as exclusions vary among carriers and this can make a big difference to you. For example, theft from an unattended vehicle may be covered under certain circumstances by one carrier but never by another. Another item to understand clearly is whether your instrument is covered while in the hands of the repair shop. Knowing these important details saves surprises when it's time to settle a claim

WHERE TO BUY INSURANCE

The most common way to place a musical-instrument policy is to contact the insurance company directly. The insurance industry in the United States is highly regulated, requiring agents to be licensed in every state in which they do business. Only a handful of carriers specialize in musical-instrument coverage and are licensed in all 50 states. In many cases insurance can be initiated over the phone with the paperwork to follow. Organizations and associations often negotiate special group coverage for their members. Group members usually deal directly with the company and pay individually, but some organizations collect the premiums from their members and pay the company as a group.

Instruments can also be insured through a valuable-property policy added to existing homeowner's coverage through your regular agent. Agents seldom write stand-alone policies, but will occasionally arrange for coverage with a specialist carrier as a courtesy to their clients.

APPRAISALS

Appraisals are not always necessary to obtain insurance, although it never hurts to have one. "Sometimes we can just call up the dealer. We know most of them, anyway," says Hershman. The replacement value of commercially made modern instruments is well-known. Clarion Associates Inc., another leader in the industry, will often accept a simple list of items and values signed by a reputable dealer with a business card attached. Appraisals are necessary, however, to establish the value of old or rare instruments, whose worth is determined by condition and the antique-instrument market.

HOW MUCH IT COSTS

As always, exact details vary, but here is a typical example. An individual instrument policy with Clarion, one of the best-known specialist carriers, carries a minimum premium of $251 per year, with no deductible, which covers values up to $25,000— you pay the same whether you are insured for $2,000 or the maximum $25,000. Hershman suggests a replacement value of $5,000 as the point at which an instrument policy becomes cost-effective.

Group affiliations can mean a substantial discount on premiums. For instance, if you happen to belong to Early Music America, one of many groups that negotiate special coverage for its members, Clarion's minimum premium would be $161 for up to $19,800 in coverage. Yearly dues for EMA are $49, so your dues and premium together still cost less than an individual policy.

A valuable-articles policy through your existing homeowner's, renter's, or even auto insurance carrier costs about $6 annually per $1,000 in value. The rate for music professionals is three times that, about $18 per year per $1,000. Even at the professional rate, this can be a bargain, especially if your instruments are of moderate value, as there is typically no minimum premium.

Playing for pay on a limited basis no longer excludes you from using homeowner's insurance. In fact, a certain amount of income doesn't even

The largest single instrument claim ever paid was $2.2 million for a Stradivari.

Only a handful of carriers specialize in musical-instrument coverage and are licensed in all 50 states.

automatically classify you as a professional, according to Barbara Southworth, a long-time insurance agent who also happens to be a musician. "Check with your homeowners' or renters' agent to determine if your policy carries a maximum income, below which your musical pursuits would be considered 'incidental,' and thus rated as non-professional," she advises. For example, her policy allowed her to earn up to $5,000 and still be considered nonprofessional, qualifying her for the lower rate.

THE ADVANTAGES OF A MUSICAL-INSTRUMENT POLICY

Musical-instrument policies are designed by experts in the field to meet the specific needs of musicians. The types of details you would have to educate yourself about and work out with a homeowner's carrier are built-in. They also offer coverage for situations common in the music world. For example, instruments loaned or entrusted to your care may be covered automatically. Damaging a colleague's instrument may be covered. And business-interruption protection could have paid the fees lost by that fiddler whose instrument broke right before the gig, and the right policy may even have covered the cost of renting a replacement while it was being repaired.

Details and special services vary quite a bit, so read up to find the package that best suits your needs. Specialists may also place insurance where other carriers would not. Heritage has partnered with XL Specialties, an A+15-rated carrier, to insure extremely valuable instruments and collections.

The largest single instrument claim ever paid was $2.2 million for a Stradivari, and that was mostly paid within 90 days, according to Hershman.

Finally, dealing with an expert who understands the musical world can avoid misunderstandings when it's time to settle a claim. This reassurance alone can be worth the price of the premium.

Southworth offers common-sense advice for getting the most out of your insurance. Good communication up front is essential. Confirm your replacement value annually and update that value when you renew your policy. A simple note from your violin dealer attached to the appraisal specifying the amount by which your instrument has increased in value is sufficient.

GET IT IN WRITING!

If you are dealing with a homeowners' policy, clarify everything in advance. Specify coverage for devaluation, define "incidental income," and work out the precise details of how the claim will be settled.

Don't wait until claim time. For example, the violinist at the beginning our story would be even more heartbroken if she discovered she had to surrender the repaired bow to the insurance company.

Gone are the days of rigid standard forms. "A carrier may be able to tailor a valuable-articles policy to meet the client's specific needs," says Southworth, emphasizing, "just get it in writing, on the policy.

"A note in the agent's file is not good enough. Get it on the policy."

A version of this chapter originally appeared in the June/July 2005 issue of Strings *magazine.*

CHAPTER 11

Time to Get Serious

Learn to cultivate good violin-shop relations

BY RICHARD WARD

As a string musician, you understand the importance of your instrument and bow. They are objects with which you form a close personal relationship and like all good relationships, it has to be cared for. Once you've invested the time, money, and effort in finding the best instrument and bow, you will need help nourishing and maintaining that relationship. Stringed instruments are finicky, even temperamental, especially as they get older. They are fragile and can be damaged if not cared for properly. They also need regular care and maintenance. This kind of care isn't something you can provide yourself; it requires the efforts of someone who is a specialist in the art and craft of violin restoration and repairs.

If you value and depend on your instrument and bow, you should put thought and care into choosing a professional to care for them, just as you would choose a doctor to care for your body. And any doctor will tell you if you take care of your body, it will take care of you.

This is where your violin shop comes in. Having a shop you can count on can provides a great sense of security. The shop staff will get to know both you and your instrument. Your violin specialist will get to know your likes and dislikes and should have a record of what strings you have used in the past.

CHOOSE A SPECIALIST

The shop you choose should meet certain standards. The luthiers who do the work on your instrument and bow should be well trained. They can receive this training in several ways. They can attend one of the violin-making schools; there are a number of these here in United States and around the world. These courses are usually followed with an extensive training period under the guidance of a master craftsman.

Some luthiers choose to bypass the school and work directly with a master maker before setting up their own shop. The master or head of the shop should oversee everything that is done. In my opinion, you can't call your business a violin shop if the work is sent out to someone else.

If you value your instrument, don't let someone work on it who repairs all kinds of other instruments (guitars, clarinets, saxophones, and drums, for example).

The staff at the front counter may not be the repair personnel themselves, but they should be knowledgeable. In most cases, they are string musicians and the front counter is the best place to learn the profession. They should be able to advise you about repairs, strings, and accessories, and be of great help in choosing an instrument or bow. I've worked behind the counter at Ifshin Violins in Berkeley, California, for 16 years and have seen every kind of instrument and all the damage that can befall them. I have tried every string and accessory and have played thousands of instruments. You should expect a good violin shop to have experienced personnel.

A good violin shop should have a respectable selection of instruments and bows available in a range of qualities and prices. If a shop has a rental program (and most seem to these days), the instruments should be well maintained and set up.

One San Francisco Bay Area teacher, Christina Meals, stresses the importance of rental instruments and insists that her students get good rentals.

Once you have chosen a violin shop you feel you can work with, what should you expect?

It's hard enough to learn to play without the handicap of a poorly set up and maintained violin. A good violin shop will take pride in both the work and the instruments that leave its business because it will stand behind what it does. Its new student instruments should be set up by the shop craftspeople, not by the factory in China or Romania or Germany where they were made, nor by the wholesaler in some other part of the country.

SHOP AROUND

There are good violin shops all over the world from which to choose. If you live in a large metropolitan area—like the San Francisco Bay Area, Los Angeles, Chicago, or New York, where there are several shops in just one building, or Paris, where there are about 20 shops on one street alone—choosing a shop shouldn't be too difficult. Just do some research.

In other areas, it will take a bit more work. The first step in finding a shop is to ask fellow musicians for recommendations. You would do this if you were looking for a doctor, plumber, or auto mechanic; why not a violin shop? Ask as many people as possible. If someone doesn't like a certain shop, ask why. After a while, a pattern will emerge. If you have just moved to a new area, ask your old shop for a referral.

Next, go to the shop for a visit. Talk to staff members and see if you will be able to work easily with them. If you are a teacher, look at their rentals and student instruments available for sale. Check their selection of strings and accessories and the professionalism of the staff. Sadly, there are people in the violin business who shouldn't be there. One thing these people seem to have in common is an ability to promote themselves. They usually have an abundance of charm, but lack real skill and training and are often downright dishonest.

If you ask enough musicians, you will find out who they are.

Once you have chosen a violin shop you feel you can work with, what should you expect? Most importantly, professionalism and communication. If you need to leave your instrument for work, you should get an explanation of what work will be done, an estimate of the cost, and a completion time. If the time required for completion seems long, remember that some work takes a great deal of time and can't be rushed, especially anything to do with varnish.

If you were undergoing major surgery, you wouldn't want the surgeon to rush so he could get to the next patient. You would want him to work slowly and carefully. So it should be with your violin. Keep in mind that as the work progresses, other problems may become evident. You should be notified if this is the case and asked before extra work is done.

Expect to pay a fair price for the work. These days, plumbers and electricians charge $100 an hour and up and most of them don't require the extensive training violin makers and craftsmen do. Your violin shop should stand behind its work, so if you have any questions about what was done, don't be afraid to ask. You should never feel intimidated.

There was a time, many years ago, when violin dealers had a tendency toward abruptness and grumpiness. I know of one dealer who, when told that a violin had lost its sound, snapped "go home and practice." Most of those folks are gone now.

SERVICES RENDERED

If you have a real emergency and need a repair done quickly, a shop should make every effort to fit you in. Do try to be understanding. The workshop may have five other emergencies waiting in line. If you are loyal customer of the shop, they may give it extra effort.

What if you are on the road, away from your home base and have an emergency? Call the shop. If the problem is something simple, the repair specialist may be able to talk you through it. If not, he or she may be able to refer you to someone trustworthy.

⌁ LET'S TALK ⌁

Communication is the key. With repairs, let the shop know what you need and discuss it openly. Explain what you would like the results to be, but don't expect miracles and don't expect involved repairs at the snap of a finger!

Allow me to offer a few suggestions.

1 When taking instruments or bows out on trial for possible purchase (any good shop should allow you to do this) bring them back by the agreed return date. Habitually keeping them out too long ties up a shop's inventory and keeps them from being shown to other customers.

2 Every teacher I know hates the cheap ($50 to $100) "Internet special" violins. The possible set-up cost may exceed the value of the instrument. Many shops won't touch them. Consider renting instead.

3 If your shop spends time helping you choose strings, chinrests, shoulder rests, or other accessories, support your local shop. Resist the temptation to buy them where they might be a bit cheaper.

4 Shops are becoming reluctant to do appraisals. If you bring an instrument to your dealer, be honest about where it came from and why you want the appraisal.

5 If you do buy an instrument from another dealer or directly from a maker, it is better to take the instrument back to the source for follow-up work and adjustment. This is especially true with makers, who tend to be very proprietary about their work. This situation can be awkward for a shop.

—R.W.

Shops often have a network of dealers they know. They may be able to call a shop where you are and make sure it can accommodate you. If there is no one to help, you may need to ship the instrument back for repair. You can get instructions on how to pack it securely.

If you are looking for an instrument or bow for yourself, I suggest that you go to your favorite shop first and try what it has. The staff should be forthcoming about specifically what each instrument is, the price, and other information. If the shop doesn't have what you are looking for, its staff may be able to find something for you from any number of sources.

If you go to other dealers and take an instrument out, don't bring it to your dealer for an appraisal. This puts your shop in a very awkward position.

Whatever is said about the instrument will have a way of getting back to the dealer, especially if it's negative, causing bad feelings at best and threats of litigation at worst. If you don't trust the dealer you've taken the instrument from, you shouldn't do business there.

DON'T FEEL INTIMIDATED

As a teacher, you should expect your shop to treat your students respectfully. Berkeley teacher Annmarie Suderman told me that students and parents can feel intimidated when they come to a shop looking for an instrument or bow mostly because of their lack of knowledge.

The shop should first make them feel welcome and comfortable, and explain everything, giving some suggestions about the process of choosing an instrument. The customer should be given prices and an explanation of trial and trade-in policies. They should be made comfortable with every step in the process.

As with any relationship, you, the client, have responsibilities as well.

A good violin shop can be your best resource. As the old advertising cliché goes: "you have a friend in the business." The violin shop is one of the few small family retail businesses that hasn't been destroyed by the big-box retailers.

Shops do have to operate on the same principles as any other business: either make enough to pay the overhead and purchase inventory, or close their doors. Support your local violin shop and it will support you!

A version of this chapter originally appeared in the June/July 2006 issue of Strings *magazine.*

Section 2

Buying Contemporary Instruments

CHAPTER 12

That First Violin

Good and even great instruments are easy to find and surprisingly affordable. There are many starter outfits—bow and case included—that cost $1,500 or less. Here are some tips on getting what you want, without hassles

BY HEATHER K. SCOTT

Students first learning the violin often start with a school fiddle or a rental from the local music shop. Parents and teachers alike know that these early days will foretell the student's future musical career. Will he learn to practice? Will she develop the discipline and desire to continue to play? If the answer is yes, most teachers will suggest purchasing that first violin, an exciting step for young musicians. I can remember the thrill of picking out my first instrument. My parents drove me to the nearest stringed-instrument dealer and we spent the day with the shopkeeper, sorting through instruments and testing each one for sound and playability. They were supportive of this first step in my musical career, but the three of us knew little about the process of choosing the best instrument for my needs. We ended up with a great outfit, one that I still have today. But looking back, I wish we'd had more help—that heavily varnished, shiny instrument I chose has lost much of the warmth and easy playability it once had.

Before you begin your search for that first violin, you'll need to look around your local shops and visit area dealers and makers. Choosing where you purchase

∼ BUYER BEWARE ∼

Some teachers receive a percentage of instrument sales from their local dealers, often as much as ten percent of the price of each instrument they recommend to their students. Many teachers put a lot of effort into helping a student search for a new instrument, and some either ask students up front for a fee for their time, or make it known that they receive commissions from shops. But teachers who keep the practice quiet are more common than you might think.

Be sure you are purchasing a violin based on good advice from a teacher, fellow player, or reliable dealer. Do research on the Internet. Make notes. Decide what price range you are going to work with, and stick with it. Dealers can be very persuasive, and there are, as one dealer pointed out to us, many instruments that look impressive but sound dull and flat, yet still carry a hefty price tag.

your new instrument is just as important as choosing the outfit itself. Buying from a maker or shop equipped to provide you with unbiased, expert advice as well as reputable instrument repair and maintenance will alleviate many setup problems.

Also remember that you are starting at the beginner's end of the scale: none of these instruments are going to compare with a custom-made bench violin. In your search it is best to compare apples to apples.

Take some time to visit the shops where you are most comfortable. Consider hiring your teacher or inviting a violinist friend to accompany you and help evaluate your options. You should know that some teachers receive a commission payment from certain dealers, or make it known that they receive commissions from shops. Knowing your teacher's practice will be helpful when considering his or her advice.

Henry Riedstra, who owns and runs a violin shop in Kitchener, Ontario, suggests visiting a violin dealer or shop that has one or more knowledgeable makers on staff. An experienced luthier, restorer, and player is far more equipped to help you or your child than a part-time store employee. Riedstra suggests actively involving the staff member in the student's shopping experience—good advice for an adult beginner as well. "Be sure to ask the shop person to play each instrument for you, as well as having your son or daughter play them. This way even an inexperienced ear will pick out the sound that is the best in the price range you can afford. You should also ask your son or daughter and the shop player to comment on the ease of response, as well as the quality of sound across all strings."

Many dealers have practice rooms available. Take in two to three instruments at a time and play the same piece of music on each. Whether you play just a basic G-major, two-octave scale, a short jig or reel, or a few bars of your favorite piece, playing consistent musical passages on each instrument will make it much easier to draw comparisons. Some dealers will even offer overnight loans of your favorite instruments. Remember to take breaks between your shopping trips, since trying too many instruments in one sitting will do nothing but confuse and frustrate you. Limit yourself to a handful of instruments and be sure to bring paper and pen to take notes. You may find it useful to create a shopping list of the qualities you seek in a violin.

Study sound and tone, setup and playability, quality of varnish, and overall craftsmanship. Look at the consistency of the entire outfit, assessing whether the

---

WHAT TO LOOK FOR WHEN
⌁ BUYING YOUR FIRST VIOLIN ⌁

1 PLAYABILITY You should be able to move from string to string freely, with an even tone across all strings.

2 TONE AND SOUND Are you looking for a violin with a warm upper register or do you prefer a bright sound in the higher strings? Test the violin's sound and be sure that you are getting the projection and tone you desire.

3 PRICE Does it fit your budget? Be sure the quality of the violin and outfit you are buying match the price tag attached. Ask teachers you trust, as well as fellow students, where they purchased their instruments and how much they paid.

4 CRAFTSMANSHIP Is the finish sprayed or brushed? Is the top hand carved or factory pressed? The craftsmanship of the violin contributes greatly to instrument's quality and potential resale value.

5 SETUP Do the pegs, chinrest, bridge, and strings fit well? You should be able to play each string clearly without brushing against other

strings—if not, it could mean your bridge or fingerboard needs adjustment. Do the pegs feel tight? Is the neck set at the correct angle? You should be able to press each string all the way down at the part of the fingerboard nearest the bridge. Your shop can take care of these problems—be sure to address them before you leave with your new instrument.

6 THE PACKAGE Is the quality consistent across the board? Check the bow (look for pernambuco bows with true horsehair, not fiberglass bows with synthetic hair). Is the case going to protect your instrument? Some dealers are open to mixing and matching their outfit options. You may find that you can purchase a better bow and safer case for the same price, or a just fraction more.

7 THE DEALER OR SHOP Check with friends, fellow musicians, and your teacher about where they like to shop for instruments and accessories. Be sure to ask about trade-in and trade-up policies. Some shops selling starter fiddles will buy back instruments and direct part of that cost to your purchase of a step-up violin.

quality of the bow and case match that of the violin. Identify and take note of the strong and weak points of each instrument, for useful comparison.

Don't concern yourself overmuch with accessories and fittings such as chin rests, tailpieces, and fine tuners. These are easily, and cheaply, replaceable, so inconsistent quality needn't be a deterrent. Keep your eyes on the fiddle itself, then consider the bow and case, and finally look at the fittings and accessories. A new set of strings, pegs, and fittings on higher-priced student violins might be a worthwhile expense and could make an otherwise good-sounding and good-looking instrument even better.

Henry Hultquist, who owns The Violin Shop in Lincoln, Nebraska, informs prospective buyers that make and model number are not always true indicators of what to expect in sound and playability. You may wish to try the same brand and model violin at several different shops to test for sound variance. "If you take six violins [with the same model number and from the same company or violin maker], there will be a noticeable difference in sound among them—sometimes a dramatic difference." Hultquist adds, "It should be noted that the same violin 'shell' may be sold under a variety of brand names."

Brand names also carry a price tag. Some companies' reputations garner a higher price that does not necessarily reflect accurately upon the instrument's value. Dealer Henry Riedstra says, "People think the more one pays for the outfit, the better the sound. But that's not always the case." Kyozo Watanabe, owner of Cremona Violin Shop, in Los Angeles, California, adds, "I have seen so many customers, as well as some teachers, buying instruments by brand name alone, and this leads to dangerous situations for the student."

The moral? Evaluate the violins you test carefully, and listen to your own opinion. With a little homework and research, the violin you find now will provide years of musical enjoyment. And the discipline and self-awareness you bring to your search may come in handy the next time you are making a large purchase—be it a car, a home, or that next violin.

A version of this chapter originally appeared in the August/September 2001 issue of Strings *magazine.*

CHAPTER 13

Stepping Up?

Time for a new axe? Tips on finding a great sound for under $5,000

BY SARAH FREIBERG

When you began to play a stringed instrument, you probably purchased an inexpensive start-up instrument or even rented your first one. You (or your parents) may not have been sure whether you'd like it, or whether you were ready to take care of it. If you were very young, you may have chosen a fractional size, and you probably outgrew that instrument in no time at all. The advantage to renting was that you could trade in the instrument for the next size up—or a better-quality model—and it would be insured in case of accidents.

But now that you've been practicing diligently for all those years and become more responsible, you may be ready to graduate to a bigger and better instrument that will help you develop as a musician. It's time to acquire your very own violin, viola, cello, or bass—your first "step-up" instrument.

A step-up instrument can be defined simply as a better-quality, better-sounding axe, most likely crafted by a contemporary maker or workshop (and usually with a better resale value).

Here are a few things to consider:

WHERE TO BEGIN

Ask your teacher for recommendations. He or she probably has helped many students find their first instrument. It may well be that the shop you rent from sells instruments as well. While some shops have a rent-to-own policy, you shouldn't plan to buy the instrument you've been renting unless you absolutely love it and can't imagine a better one. Yanbing Chen, co-owner of Goronok String Instruments in Cleveland, suggests that the buyer beware: "One thing to watch out for is that some music stores will lock you in to the instrument you are renting. That's not good."

These aren't always the best quality instruments, he adds, and may not be in pristine condition—a series of renters can be hard on an instrument. On the other hand, many string shops have a policy that lets you apply a percentage of the rental fee toward the purchase of another instrument—after you've been renting for a predetermined period.

Even if your teacher suggests potential shops, there are a couple of things to keep in mind. "It is most important to feel comfortable in searching for an instrument you'll like," says Susan Horkan, former sales manager for Johnson String Instrument in Newton Center, Massachusetts. "You should be able to communicate well with the dealers, as well as feel that you can trust them."

Violinist and teacher Maria Benotti puts it another way: "You want to know your dealer. You want someone to be fair about it."

You also want a shop that stands behind its work, so it doesn't hurt to ask around. "You want to make sure that the general workmanship is sound," Chen says. "If it turns out that there is a problem with the instrument, you want to make sure that the shop will cover it." At the Goronok shop, for example, if there's a flaw in workmanship or material of an instrument purchased there, it's covered for life.

And while it's fine to search far and wide for just the right instrument, consider buying close to home. Doug Cox, a Vermont-based violin maker, agrees that "what you are paying for is the service."

Music schools are another good place to look for instruments. Benotti teaches in the preparatory division of the New England Conservatory, and reports that "a lot of the conservatory kids need to upgrade. I encourage my [students] to look on the board at NEC for instruments. As the older kids upgrade, my kids benefit. It's fortunate to be at a school."

WHAT TO ASK

While Horkan notes, "Most prospective buyers don't have a lot of information about purchasing instruments, and there really isn't much out there," she does feel that it's helpful to know the structural parts of the instrument. Also, find out the condition of the instruments that you are looking at—particularly the antiques. The health of an instrument is crucial. If the instrument is new, research the luthier or the company that made it. Horkan considers her role as seller to include educating prospective buyers in what to look for: the types of instruments available in their price range; the pros and cons of contemporary and antique instruments; and the types of sound available.

The handy Rough Guide book series (www.roughguides.com/music) is a good place to start—and at a very good price. You're about to make a significant purchase, so it's wise to know as much as you can. The series includes the *Rough Guide to Violin & Viola* as well as the *Rough Guide to Cello*, both of which offer plenty of helpful tips. The same publisher also offers a series of instrument tip books.

HOW MUCH WILL IT COST?

Prices of step-up instruments range from $1,500 to $5,000. Although you may think that a higher price means a better instrument, sometimes a premium is attached for details such as fancier fittings, more intricate inlay, and other niceties that don't necessarily affect the tone of the instrument. There are some very good quality instruments at the lower end of the spectrum. Define what your upper limit is before you go shopping for your new instrument—and remember there will be plenty to look at in each of the price ranges.

Be sure to check the Violin Pricing Guide in the *Strings* Buyer's Guide for contact and pricing information on numerous makers and their going rates. (The Guide is available online at www.stringsmagazine.com.) Many musicians even have had custom instruments made within these lower- to mid-range prices.

The larger the instrument, the more you pay. Violas cost more than violins, and cellos are higher still. "You should expect to pay at least $1,500 for an acceptable-quality cello," Chen says. "I wouldn't go below that, unless you are ready to deal with other problems. You want good quality that will last."

Also, the age of the instrument makes a difference in that price. As Horkan points out: "antique instruments usually command a higher price. And the inexpensive antiques are disappearing. I recently attended an instrument auction in New York, and found that the low-end antiques were commanding surprisingly high prices."

Since older instruments have been around for a while, they also may have more problems. It is extremely important to know the condition of an older instrument before you purchase it, otherwise you may be spending additional time and money for repairs.

The good news is, as Horkan puts it, "There are so many great contemporary makers [and] terrific new instruments that are reliable, consistent, and structurally sound."

Chen adds, "A lot of people think that older instruments are better, and a better value. This is not really true except for much older, much higher-priced, and well-documented instruments. But for students who want a good-quality instrument, a cello manufactured in Germany 40 years ago can't compete in sound or workmanship with the new instruments now available. The new instruments sound so much better for less cost."

One reason for this is the growth of the global market. Claire Givens, owner of Claire Givens Violins in Minneapolis, points out that in the under-$4,000 range "there has been a vast change in the marketplace."

These days, the labor costs are lower in the Eastern Bloc countries, she adds, and that can translate into better deals for US and Canadian buyers.

And then there is Asia.

"The Chinese revolution of instruments has brought incredible quality to the market," Cox says. "I think it's great for the future of string playing. From my perspective, there will be more students who go further, stick with it, and will be my clients later on."

Most foreign-made step-up instruments in this price range are crafted by a group of people rather than just a single maker. The Goronok shop, for example, has set up workshops in Mexico and China where the instruments are fashioned. One person makes the scrolls, another the plates of the instruments, and yet another puts them together. Then they are sent to the shop in Cleveland for varnishing, finishing, and setup.

Chen notes that "workshop instruments were very common throughout the centuries. Violin makers would often employ apprentices. The maker/artist is a new phenomenon, one that has grown in the last century, particularly in America."

SET YOUR STANDARDS

Choosing an instrument is a very personal endeavor, and it takes time. Make sure to allot at least an hour or two when you first visit a shop, and don't buy on impulse. Plan to take instruments home. Play them for your teacher. Visit many shops to compare. Cox says not to worry if the process takes a few months. After all, you're purchasing an instrument that will be your "voice," one that you will hopefully keep for a long time. Most shops let you take instruments for a week or two for a trial. Try to take home two contrasting instruments so that you can compare them over time.

"Although everyone has different tastes," says Horkan, "there are certain things all players can look for in an instrument: responsiveness, ease of playing, evenness of tone from string to string and throughout the range of the instrument. Some players prefer a mellow sound. However, I try to steer students toward an open, clean sound. Comfort is extremely important. It really works both ways, though: If a student is comfortable with an instrument, he or she will pull out a better sound—and if he or she likes the sound, the instrument feels more comfortable."

Horkan explains that an instrument's appeal to a player really depends on personal taste. "The same instrument and bow can sound completely different with different players," she says.

Learning to recognize what you're looking for, and how to describe it, is crucial. "A significant part of the search is developing vocabulary," says Cox. "In fact, I don't know how much my vocabulary matches others in business. What do 'dark' and 'light' mean, for example? A shared vocabulary speeds the process along."

As you try out instruments, don't worry about the labels—just listen for the sound you want. "I want [students] to try a lot of instruments," says Benotti, "When they go out they haven't a clue—but they quickly learn what they like. In the process of trying and experimenting, they find out what they want."

THE RIGHT FIT

Usually, between you and your teacher, you'll know when you find the right instrument. As Horkan points out, the instrument should feel comfortable. "In helping a player choose an instrument, I look for verbal and physical cues," she says. "I'm aiming for when a player says, 'I just love this instrument.' Sometimes I can see players relax with a particular instrument—and I know they've found the right one. Sometimes I may notice that they tense up with one instrument and I'll make sure to communicate that to them."

This brings up another issue: standard size of instruments. If you choose an instrument that's a little different (larger or smaller), you'll end up adjusting to it—but it may be hard to readjust when you move on to your next instrument. Cox says that "you become used to a nonstandard instrument—and your technique will end up conforming to it." Benotti recently went through the process of finding a cello for her son. They liked a particular instrument that had unusually sloping shoulders, she says, but were told by cello colleagues that it would be hard to adjust to, particularly for a child. So they continued their search—ultimately finding the perfect one.

If you've been renting, you may need not only an instrument, but a bow and case, too. Don't forget to reserve some of your money for this. Some shops offer package deals. Johnson String Instrument offers violin outfits, for example, with a hard Bobelock case and a choice of either a carbon fiber or a wood bow. Goronok will add a bow and case for an extra $500. Givens encourages people to pick the instrument separately from the bow. It's a good idea to get to know your instrument and then find a bow that matches it well.

Horkan suggests that "before you leave the shop, make sure you know how to care for the instrument. You want to protect your investment. You need to learn when to bring the instrument back to the shop. For example, if your bridge gets knocked and becomes improperly adjusted in relation to the sound post, you could find the instrument cracking [in the future]."

Hopefully, you are getting an instrument that will grow with you and serve your needs for many years. And while you may not want to think of this now, eventually you may want to sell the instrument. Be sure to inquire about the trade-in policy before you finalize your purchase. Ask whether the shop will take the instrument back on consignment, or as credit toward a future purchase.

While really great old instruments appreciate in value (which is why most players can't afford an old Italian instrument), for the most part the lower-end instruments won't go up that much. This isn't always the case, however, especially when considering the growing number of quality contemporary makers infusing the market with good-quality mid-priced instruments.

But no matter the route you choose, if you take care of your instrument, you will most likely get a return on your investment when you step up to an even better one in the future.

A version of this chapter originally appeared in the April 2003 issue of Strings *magazine.*

CHAPTER 14

Made to Order

Spotlight on the special duet formed by musicians
and those who build their dream works

BY DAVID TEMPLETON

t begins when a musician decides to acquire a brand-new instrument. Perhaps
she dreams of a violin that comfortably fits her unique needs regarding sound
and size. She may be seeking a replica of a legendary cello, or an exact copy of a
treasured family heirloom. Or a violist may desire a bow that is an aesthetic match
to the color and luster of a particular instrument.

Our ambitious musician can certainly decide to go shopping, haunting the
auction houses or settling for whatever happens to be hanging on some music
store's wall. Or, if feeling especially adventurous, the musician might take the leap,
boldly choosing to have his or her dream instrument custom made.

The collaboration between the stringed-instrument player and the skilled
luthier—joined together in the creation, from scratch, of a custom musical
instrument—is a peculiarly intimate one, requiring a level of communication and
mutual trust that is paralleled in few other buyer/seller relationships. As violinist
Duane Voskuil puts it, remembering the violin made for him by New Jersey
instrument maker Colin Langman, "There must be enough of an interpersonal

exchange to develop respect, to begin to form an understanding of what the player wants—and what the maker can do."

Remarkably, it seems that every such collaboration ends up with its own descriptive metaphor. Some talk of their experience as if it were the playing of an improvised duet, or an arranged marriage between two strangers. To others, it is like giving birth to a child, or stepping through a doorway into a whole new world of musical appreciation.

Often, it seems, food is involved.

Whatever the metaphor, there's no doubt that creating a custom instrument demands a unique form of synergy that's frequently rewarding for musicians and makers alike.

EAT, DRINK, AND DO LUTHERIE

"The collaboration between the musician and the maker is firstly about the mechanics of the instrument," explains Clifford Roberts, "and secondly about getting to know and understand the needs of the musician." An accomplished luthier with a busy shop in Philadelphia, Roberts has built more than 250 instruments over the last 29 years, averaging ten to 12 instruments a year—many of them custom jobs. "The third part of the collaboration," Roberts adds, "is getting to know each other. Long phone conversations are always part of the process. Sharing good food, good wine, and good conversation is always a plus."

For Roberts—and a good number of other luthiers, it turns out—wining and dining is a major part of any custom instrument-building process.

Recounting a successful collaboration with visionary cellist Fred Sherry—for whom Roberts once built a custom five-string cello—the luthier describes not only the lengthy discussions concerning size, style, and quality of sound, but the gourmet meals the two of them shared whenever Sherry visited to look in on the progress of his instrument.

One such meal, which Roberts himself prepared—"It was a Szechuan dinner with spring rolls, Taipan ham, crispy smoked duck, and eggplant," he recalls in detail—took place when Sherry's visit coincided with the luthier's birthday. The cello, at that point, was finished but for the varnish, and—along with dessert—Sherry was treated to his first opportunity to play the new instrument. When Sherry returned several weeks later to claim the completed cello, it was during the Passover holiday. Says Roberts, "My family's good fortune was to have Fred perform for us on his finished product. Thank goodness the cello was—in Fred's and everyone else's opinion—a great success."

Another successful collaboration also involved food—and more. The musician was New York's Toby Appel, world renowned master of the violin and the viola, a frequent NPR commentator, and for the past 18 years an instructor at the Juilliard School of Music. Appel also is an accomplished gourmand, the one-time private chef to painter Georgia O'Keefe. Appel and Roberts first met after a concert at which Appel had performed on a rare viola, made in 1705 by Hieronymus Amati II. Originally built as tenor viola with a back length of about 18 inches, it had been refit with a back length of 17 3/8, and the center of the top had been cut out to reduce the instrument's width. It was, says Roberts, "One of the finest instruments you will ever hope to hear." He had to have a closer look. Recalls Appel, "Cliff came up to me and said, 'Man, that's some viola. I'd love to take some measurements of that some time.'"

The ice thus broken, they arranged to meet again to take the measurements—and to share a meal—and the bonding was complete.

"Food is very important to me," admits Appel with a chuckle. "If I'm going to commission an instrument from someone, and going to be spending a lot of time with him, it really helps if he happens to be a good cook."

Eventually, Appel commissioned a copy of the Amati, and Roberts persuaded the musician to roll up his sleeves and help. "I had him do a lot of the schlep-work," Roberts jokes, describing the process of building the viola with Appel, an experience that, working on and off, lasted about a year, including 12 months marked by what Roberts calls, "many interesting days and nights spent working, eating, and drinking good wines."

"It was a lot of fun," Appel agrees. "Cliff told me I really ought to know what it's like to make an instrument, and now I know. He let me make a lot of stupid mistakes. Now I'm the proud owner of a Roberts-Appel viola. Or maybe it's an Appel-Roberts. We've never decided.

"But it's a magnificent instrument."

IT HELPS TO BE A PEOPLE PERSON

As a professor of English and American folklore and the dean of the University of New Mexico's University College, Peter White has little spare time. Miraculously, he has managed to build a stellar reputation as a first-class luthier. In the Albuquerque shop he shares with long-time violin-making partner Ken Keppler, White has crafted over 200 violins, violas, and cellos, many of which are now played in symphony orchestras throughout the country. And he has earned a name as one of only a handful of makers producing custom five-string violins favored by country and bluegrass fiddlers.

"At this point in my life," he says, "what's most important is the act of making something together with someone else. That's why I enjoy collaborations. It's a doorway into establishing a friendship on a much more personal, and a deeper artistic level, than what you can do by working by yourself."

Of the art of lutherie, White admits, "It's often a lonely occupation, working by yourself in a shop. And though you can't form a relationship with everyone who comes into your shop, when you do have a friendship opportunity, you have to seize it."

Such a friendship grew out of his years-long collaboration with Peter Ostroushko. It began when the acclaimed musician—known for his work with the St. Paul Chamber Orchestra, Bob Dylan, Bobby McFerrin, and Emmylou Harris—called White to commission a five-string violin. The friendship deepened during the summer that the two worked side-by-side in White's shop, improvising a way to use violin-making techniques to build a custom mandolin. They've grown so fraternally supportive, in fact, that according to White, the two even quit smoking together.

⌐ THE ROMANCE OF LUTHERIE ⌐

Joseph Grubaugh was majoring in theory and composition at the University of the Pacific in the early 1970s, when he first set foot inside a luthier's shop. It was a life-changing moment. "Everything was so 3-D!" exclaims Grubaugh, describing the shop. "There were instruments in pieces. Chunks of wood carved into amazing shapes. People using varnish made from 17th-century ingredients. I couldn't *help* myself. I wanted to be a part of that!" Thirty-plus years later, Grubaugh is now very much a part of that.

The violins he creates with Sigrun Seifert, his partner in life and lutherie, are widely regarded as among the finest in the world.

Says violist Toby Appel, "Joe Grubaugh and Sigrun Seifert are, quite simply, at the top of the heap."

Mark Summer, cellist with the Turtle Island String Quartet, agrees. His cello—a Servais Strad copy, with willow back and sides—was made by Grubaugh and Seifert in 1997. "These people are so knowledgeable, and so in love with the making," he says. "The way they do things, by following the leads of the great old makers, incorporates the

lessons taught by the greats along with all the science that modern makers have learned."

Summer, who admits that as a young musician he always assumed he'd play nothing but old instruments, recalls that when he began looking at new cellos, he wanted something with "a big, big sound and a beautiful tone." He also wanted a strong, durable instrument that could handle his murderous touring schedule. "I play all over the world," he says, "so my cello would have to be strong." He already knew Grubaugh and Seifert, having met them years before when they did some repair work for him. "I play classical music, I play jazz, I play modern music," he says. "I needed a very versatile instrument, and that's what they gave me."

Within their medium-size, maximally crammed workshop on an inconspicuous tree-lined residential street in Petaluma, California, Grubaugh and Seifert build and refurbish dozens of violins, violas, and cellos each year, working in the Italian tradition they learned in Los Angeles under the tutelage of the late

"Making a custom instrument is a four-cornered experience," White says. "There's the musician, the audience, the instrument—and me. The main part of that equation," he adds, "is not the instrument I make. It's the person I'm making the instrument for."

SCIENCE MEETS ART

Barbara Theobald, of Chelsea, Massachusetts, is a professional microbiologist. Or was, until she switched careers in the late 1980s, giving up the science of microbes for the very different science of lutherie. "Violin making," she says, "tends to bring a lot of the sciences together, and at the same time it's a very exacting art form. So, for me, it's been the best of both worlds."

A graduate of the violin-making program at the North Bennet Street School in Boston, Theobald has since carved out a name for herself as a methodical maker with a good head for logistical problem solving. It's a description that matches

Hans Weisshaar. A visitor to the shop might be inspired to utter such words as "magical" or "enchanting," in part because Grubaugh and Seifert's shop can be reached only by traversing a garden path, past a moss-covered fountain, and over a bridge under which runs the tiniest of streams. Inside are at least three quartets' worth of instruments, in varying stages of development. A four-foot-tall stack of wood bits—spruce, maple, willow, and poplar—stands by the stairs. "Expensive kindling," Seifert calls it. And pinned over one work table is a photo of Hans Weisshaar himself. "He stares down at me whenever I'm doing a neck," says Grubaugh.

Of Seifert's own first encounter with the lure of lutherie, she tells of being raised in a family where music was always highly valued. "I grew up playing an instrument," she says. Still, the life-changing moment did not come for her until she entered the violin shop where her brother's instrument was being mended. "I was so curious," she adds. "I just stood there, looking and looking, thinking, 'This is great.' On the way home, my brother said, 'There's the profession for you, Sigrun. Once you learn how, you can make me a violin.'"

She learned violin-making while at school in Mittenwald, Germany, home to legendary luthiers, and later moved to Los Angeles for her apprenticeship with Weisshaar. It was in Weisshaar's shop, in fact, that Seifert met Grubaugh. "I thought, when I first gave in to my desire to make violins," she says, with a laugh, "that I'd be living the life of a hermit. Occasionally interrupted by someone giving me money, of course. Instead, I spend my days making violins with Joe, which is never boring. I get to see the tears in the eyes of a musician when she sees her new cello for the first time. It's easy to be happy with a life like that."

Grubaugh agrees, adding that lutherie is the perfect combination of intellectual and artistic pursuits, enveloping, as it does, the disciplines of art, history, science, music, and math. "There's everything happening in a violin," Grubaugh says. "A violin is in constant danger of falling into chaos. As a luthier, you bring order to the chaos, but change one thing, and chaos reclaims the instrument.

"What's not exciting about facing that every day of your life?"

—D.T.

what Paul Perley, a Vermont cellist with his own thriving instrument-repair business, had been looking for.

"I'd been trying to find an American maker, in relative proximity to Vermont, to make instruments of my own models," he explains. Specifically, Perley needed a maker willing to adhere stringently to the technical specifications he wanted. Finding such a person within driving distance was not an easy task. Ultimately, Perley saw Theobald's name in the Marketplace listings of *Strings* magazine. Taking a chance, he gave her a call.

"I just lucked out on finding her," he says. "Most new makers want more freedom than I was willing to give. I mean, I was very specific about what I wanted. From the moment I first talked to Barbara on the phone, it seemed that this sort of thing might actually work."

As Theobald recalls, "It was obvious that Paul knew exactly what he wanted." Perley owned an unlabeled, early-20th-century cello that was suited to his own needs. He wanted it duplicated down to the length and width, also to match the unusual aesthetic quality created by the cello's uniquely shaped bouts and the placement of the f-holes. "I was on the end of a long line of specifications," says Theobald, "and it was my job to hold up the workmanship side of those specifications."

She made the journey from Chelsea to Perley's own repair shop in Worcester, Vermont. "We talked most of the day," says Perley. "We went through piles of wood." Among Perley's stipulations was that the cello be made with a poplar back, which Perley feels gives the instrument a richer sound, and also requires less break-in time than other woods. Theobald had never worked with this type of wood before, but was eager to experiment. Perley provided the wood from his stockpile, Theobald took pages of notes, loaded up, and returned to her shop.

Four months later, the cello was ready.

"I played it and it was wonderful," Perley says. "She was very accurate. Right on the money. And it's a beautiful instrument. I couldn't be happier with the arrangement. Right now she's working on a second cello for me."

"It was my pleasure to be part of this collaboration with Paul," says Theobald, "and I hope that with each new instrument, we can learn a little more about what makes a great cello."

INTERACTIVE BOW MAKING

"A magnificent piece of wood!" That is how musician Toby Appel describes the Peccatte-style viola bow custom-made for him by then New York (now Portland, Oregon) bow maker Michael Yeats. "The bows that Michael makes are extraordinary,"

Appel comments, explaining that when he approached Yeats to construct a new bow, they spent a lot of time talking about wood. "Michael can hold a piece of wood in his hand and know immediately what kind if bow it will make."

And exactly how it will sound.

"As a bow maker," says Yeats, "you are interacting with the player and the instrument. After all, the bow is the thing in between the two."

While pointing out that the essential design of the bow has been unchanged since the early 1800s—most of Yeats' bows are copies of the work of 19th-century makers—he does feel there is plenty of room for collaboration between bow makers and musicians, mainly in the areas of aesthetics and comfort.

"A bow maker must first access the nature of the instrument they are attempting to match," Yeats explains, "and choose wood that will complement that instrument." For example, a bright instrument, he says, will require a bow that brings out a warmer quality, while a darker instrument wants a bow that brings more clarity and focus.

Then, of course, says Yeats, a player will have physical requirements, perhaps wanting "a fluid, supple bow, like a Tourte, with a cushion that wraps around the string, or they may prefer bows like those made by Eugene Sartory, bows that are strong and focused."

This, Yeats suggests, is when the collaboration really gets interesting.

He describes the bow he made for Jerry Grossman, coprinciple cellist of the New York Metropolitan Opera. Once it was completed, Grossman noticed an "edginess, or crunch" near the frog. Deciding that more cushion from the frog through the first quarter of the bow was called for, Yeats made the change. "It solved the sound problem," he reports. "That kind of interaction is what it's all about. I learned something more about 'crunch,' and the subtleties of the bow— and he got a bow that did everything he wanted it to."

ADVANCED ERGONOMICS

"I have small hands," states violinist Aubri McVey, currently studying at Butler College in Indianapolis. An enthusiastic musician with tastes that run from symphony and chamber music to jazz and folk, McVey has been performing for years in various small ensembles, with the Butler Symphony Orchestra, and as a soloist on a number of CDs. Over that time, she has played numerous violins, but, she says, "They're almost always uncomfortable. I have trouble reaching some of the notes on a normal-size violin. Most instruments felt like a club in my hands." There was one violin that met her needs: the beautiful Nicola Gagliano owned by

HOW TO CHOOSE
⤳ AN INSTRUMENT MAKER ⤳

While the musicians interviewed for this article are active professional players and recording artists, it's important to note that *anyone* can commission a custom-made instrument or bow at a wide range of prices. There are a number of things to consider before committing to this purchase, however. For instance, while a particular instrument maker might be best to actually construct the instrument, you should determine whether that same person will be readily available or even close enough to handle repairs. Are you prepared to take this dream work to a repair person closer to home?

Fortunately, there are a lot of resources that can assist you before making your final decision. The annual *Strings* magazine Buyer's Guide — available on-line at www.stringsmagazine.com or at newsstands throughout July and August—lists hundreds of luthiers in North America and Europe. And the American Federation of Violin and Bow Makers offers an extensive listing of instrument and bow makers in the United States and Canada. So shop around.

Meanwhile, here are four important questions you should ask before commissioning a custom instrument:

How much will it cost?

Costs vary widely from maker to maker, and are determined by everything from quality of craftsmanship to the types of materials to the level of demand for that maker's work. Ask up front what the exact costs are so you won't be shocked down the line. While there is no established industry guideline, Bill Babcock of Claire Givens Violins in Minneapolis says, you can expect to pay about $7,500 to $15,000 for a custom-made violin; $9,000 to $18,000 for a viola; and $10,000 to $23,000 for a cello. A custom-made bow will cost about $2,000 to $4,000. "When purchasing instruments of this caliber," he adds, "you can expect instruments with good response, projection, and tonal color. The details may vary slightly depending on the maker and model, but any instrument in this range should have these qualities. Other things to look for are the quality of the wood, craftsmanship, and varnish."

How long will it take?

Like prices, waiting time is different from maker to maker. While some shops might be able to produce a new instrument in one to two months, many excellent luthiers need six months, sometimes more. You will need to consider that your new instrument could be held up for some time.

Do you have references?

It's perfectly acceptable, when shopping for an instrument maker, to ask for references, say, three to five accessible people who own that maker's instruments. Reputable makers will freely offer that information.

Call the previous clients and chat to see if they were happy with the process and the results. What the heck: Ask if you can come over and play the instrument.

Do I get visiting rights?

Most makers encourage customers to come by from time to time during the making of an instrument. You'll learn what has gone into your new work of art and the maker will know you're getting what you want.

—D.T.

McVey's teacher, Larry Shapiro. Crafted in 1722 by Gagliano, whose work is often mistaken for that of Stradivari, the violin's outline was perfect for McVey, and the neck—worn down from decades of playing—was smaller than usual, exactly the right width to suit her hands. When she finally set out to commission an instrument that was ergonomically suited to her needs, it was that specific Gagliano that served as her model.

But the violin was in pieces at the time.

Shapiro had hired Indiana luthier Mark Russell to do a complete resuscitation of the Gagliano, and the instrument was only half finished. Approaching Russell, McVey discussed the possibility of constructing an exact duplicate of the old violin. Russell leaped at the challenge, eager to find a way to meet McVey's physical and musical requirements.

"The task," admits Russell, "was a bit overwhelming. She was looking for a dark sound that was rich, immediately responsive, and full of overtones." After watching her play, Russell took measurements and began to map out the best way to construct the new violin, tailoring the copy to suit her body and playing style. Though the Gagliano's string length is slightly shorter than most violins, to accommodate McVey's needs, Russell decided to make the string length even shorter.

The commission was made in the summer of 1999 and completed in November of 2000. During the intervening months, McVey exercised what she calls her "visiting rights," dropping in often to watch the process unfold.

"I can't tell you how much this has taught me about the instrument I play," she says. "Now, when I play, I have so much more appreciation for what the maker goes through. I'd studied physics and acoustics, but to see the process from the moment my violin was just two blocks of wood through till when Mark cut it out, hollowed out the top, right up to the final varnishing—it was like watching my baby grow up!"

As for Russell, he feels it's one of his most successful instruments, one that sounded as good—if not better—than the violin it was copied from. And McVey has nothing but pride for her custom-made violin.

"It's been fantastic!" she exclaims. "The longer I play it the better it gets."

A version of this chapter originally appeared in the April 2002 issue of Strings *magazine.*

CHAPTER 15

What If You Can't Commission?

Finding an instrument that's already made

BY MARK SUMMER

ommissioning an instrument is one way to acquire an instrument built by your favorite maker. But it's also risky. What if you don't like the result? Suddenly you're in a very awkward position indeed. Of course, this works both ways—the maker's reputation, self-esteem, and desire to please are on the line as well.

As the cellist of the improvisational Turtle Island String Quartet, I had long wrestled with my tubby, somewhat difficult-to-play English cello, made in 1800 by Charles Harris I. In the fall of 1996, I considered having my friends Joseph Grubaugh and Sigrun Seifert of Petaluma, California, make a new cello for me. During a visit when I watched them at work on what was to become their next instrument, I asked if they would accept my commission.

Grubaugh's response surprised me. "We don't like to work on commissions," he told me, denouncing them as "prenuptial arrangements." He added, "It's much too stressful. We like to be free to make the instruments we want to make, and we don't want to be in the position of having someone buy an instrument that they're not happy with." After my initial surprise, I realized my friends' policy made a lot of sense for them—and for me, as both friend and potential buyer. Struck by their sincerity and integrity, I found myself even more intrigued by the idea of owning one of their cellos and told Grubaugh that I would like to be added to their waiting list.

After several months, Grubaugh and Seifert finished the cello I had watched them working on and allowed me to take it to play in concert. My immediate pleasure in its rich sound and physical beauty was dampened by the knowledge that someone else was ahead of me on the waiting list. That person had the first right of refusal—in other words, I would only get a chance at the cello if that player didn't want it. My decision was thus made a bit complex: while trying to decide if the instrument was right for me, I knew I'd have to wait to find out if it was even available.

While I sweated the decision, the cello was sold and I was back to square one. But I was next on the waiting list. Grubaugh and Seifert make two cellos a year—priced in the $30,000 range, or more—and soon started making another instrument, a "brother" to the last one (which by now had received a gold medal from the Violin Society of America for craftsmanship and tone). This instrument, like the one before it, was inspired by the "Servais" and "Castelbarco" Stradivaris, with willow used for the back and ribs. Each instrument's spruce top featured prominent knots. I was quite excited by the boldness and clarity my friends had achieved in that first cello—they succeeded in creating a contemporary instrument that paid homage to the great Strad cellos yet had a sound and look all its own.

As I played this new cello, I was again impressed. But this time I knew that the decision to buy or not was mine. Was this cello as good as the first one? A tough call. I took the cello home and tried to live with this new sound that was coming out of "me."

Making a decision proved to be frustrating and energy-intensive. I seemed to be feeling buyer's remorse even before I bought the instrument—not surprising, really, considering the time, money, and effort involved. While it seems to be the norm to allow prospective buyers to keep an instrument for two weeks, I needed more time, and Grubaugh and Seifert agreed to give me another week. I decided to call several colleagues, have them play the new cello, and gather their opinions about it. The response of a knowledgeable cellist living in San Francisco tipped the scales for me. Hearing the cello played by a consummate professional and receiving her assurances that it was the finest contemporary cello she had ever played calmed me down. I bought the cello, and feel I finally have what I'd been searching for: an instrument that completely supports my varied needs as a performing and recording artist.

Unquestionably, whether you commission an instrument or put yourself on a waiting list for a noncommissioned one, it helps to establish a relationship with the maker you choose. Both Grubaugh and Seifert were very sensitive to my needs and took the time to teach me about the instrument-making process. I saw the cello in its naked, unvarnished state, and it was thrilling to witness the linen linings and the hand-stamped label being glued in.

In the end, I had more of an appreciation for the care, knowledge, and workmanship that went into the instrument, and with that knowledge I feel confident that my new cello is the right one for me.

A version of this chapter originally appeared in the November 1997 issue of Strings *magazine.*

CHAPTER 16

Modern Sound

Contemporary instruments face a lingering, if mild,
prejudice among symphony players and conductors

BY JAMES REEL

To the distress of living instrument makers and the musicians who patronize them, the myth won't die: Conductors sometimes ban contemporary instruments from their orchestras. "I can't say that I know so-and-so hates modern instruments, but I have heard that story," says violinist Jaime Laredo, who has soloed with enough top orchestras to have heard a tale or two.

Nobody seems to be able to report with any certainty that a particular conductor disciplined or banned a particular player for fouling his orchestra with some horrid modern instrument. Could this be a mere urban legend? The surest way to find out is by asking some conductors.

Unfortunately, of the seven leading American maestros we tried to contact, only the Seattle Symphony's Gerard Schwarz agreed to speak out on the topic. And he has plenty to say. "I'm very proud to have some of the great, historical instruments in the orchestra that we do," he begins. "But I've heard instruments made in the latter part of the 20th century that are phenomenal, and I've seen new bows as beautifully crafted as any Tourte you can find. If there's a prejudice that unless you have an old Italian it's useless to try to get into a major orchestra, it's just not true.

"Many players function very well on modern instruments—thank God, *very* well."

Is Schwarz more accommodating than some of his colleagues? Listen to Christopher Reuning, owner of Boston's Reuning and Son Violins and a partner in Tarisio auctions in New York City. "I've never heard a conductor say no to new instruments," says Reuning, who maintains many instruments for members of the Boston Symphony Orchestra. "But I've heard stories where somebody's playing an audition, and the conductor says, 'You can have the job, but you'll have to play on a better instrument.'

"And there are tenured musicians who've owned a better instrument, but decided to downgrade it and take the money, and they run into all sorts of opposition."

Reuning hastens to add that he believes top-quality modern instruments should not be banned. "I'm not suggesting that an old violin is always better than a new violin," he says. "There are new instruments that can hold their own in any orchestra. In the 1970s and '80s, the Philadelphia Orchestra had many players who played Peresson instruments, and that was looked upon favorably by the organization. But for the most part, when a BSO player is trying to buy a

✎ IN TOUCH WITH THE TIMES ✐

Which top players perform and record with contemporary instruments? That's a tricky question; it's easier to list those who merely own contemporary instruments, while preferring 18th-century instruments for most concerts and recording sessions. Nigel Kennedy, for instance, has used a Scott Cao violin, but he seems to do most of his work on a 1736 Guarneri.

Although Jaime Laredo's main instrument is a 1717 Stradivari, he also owns two "terrific" violins by Fayetteville, Arizona's Terry Michael Borman. "In my home I have a complete quartet of his instruments, including a viola, and my wife [Sharon Robinson, like her husband a member of the Kalichstein-Laredo-Robinson Trio] has a cello made

by him. I have used both violins and his viola in concerts many, many times, and I played his viola in a couple of the piano quartet recordings I did with Isaac Stern, Yo-Yo Ma, and Emmanuel Ax."

Other clients claimed by Borman include Pinchas Zukerman, Pamela Frank, Jose-Luis Garcia, and Cho-Liang Lin. "His instruments are wonderful," says Lin, who also owns—in addition to his Giuseppe Guarneri del Gesu—a Samuel Zygmuntowicz violin. "I played [the Zygmuntowicz] on my 2001 tour to Australia and Asia, and nobody noticed the difference," says Lin.

Says Laredo, "I did a tour last year with the Emerson String Quartet, and Phil Setzer and David

[classic] couple-hundred-thousand dollar violin on his salary, the BSO helps finance it."

Major orchestras will go to even greater expense to populate their ranks with Guarneris, Guadagninis, and Montagnanas. Bing Wang, associate concertmaster of the Los Angeles Philharmonic, plays a 1777 Guadagnini on loan from the orchestra since 1995, the year after she joined the group. Before that, as principal second violin in the Cincinnati Symphony, she'd used her own instrument, a 1924 Luigi Rovatti, made in Buenos Aires. "It sounds pleasant under my ear, but it doesn't project as well [as the Guadagnini], and it doesn't have the same sweetness," she says. "But it's very responsive and pleasant to play."

Even so, her goal is eventually to acquire an old Italian instrument of her own.

Yet the LA Philharmonic's generosity in lending classic instruments to key players shouldn't be taken as a sign that modern instruments are verboten. "In our orchestra, I'm seeing more contemporary instruments, little by little," says Wang. "Several people *sometimes* use them, and a number of players have them as their first instruments—maybe five or six people in the violin section."

KEEP A SPARE

Check the websites of contemporary violin makers, and you'll find several boasting that their violins are in the hands of current or former members of the orchestras of

---

Finckel played Zygmuntowicz instruments. They were extraordinary; they sounded as good as anything I've heard."

Among other clients listed by Zygmuntowicz are Nicholas Kitchen and Ruggero Allifranchini of the Borromeo Quartet, the late Isaac Stern, Roman Totenberg, Walter Trampler, Daniel Heifetz, Dylana Jensen, Daniel Phillips of the Orion Quartet, and Ruggiero Ricci.

Ricci's name turns up on several contemporary makers' client lists. For example, he owns an Alf copy of his own Guarneri. Similarly, Elmar Oliveira has an exact Curtin and Alf copy of his 1726 "Lady Stretton" Guarneri. "He raves about it," says Lin.

Some other celebrities claimed by living makers:

Members of the Hagen and Stradivari quartets use instruments by Joseph Curtin.

Kenneth Sillito of the Academy of St. Martin in the Fields has used a Harris & Sheldon violin for more than 10 years.

Moes & Moes instruments have fallen into the hands of Hilary Hahn, Nobuko Imai, Ida Kavafian, Yo-Yo Ma, Scott Nickrenz, and Isaac Stern (a viola, in his case).

Maxim Vengerov used a Masa Inokuchi "cornerless" violin to record his music-video version of the "Meditation" from Massenet's Thaïs.

And Lawrence Wilke cellos have been played by Aldo Parisot and Janos Starker.

"I'm encouraging young players who don't have a million-dollar budget or wealthy patrons to support them to look into modern instruments," says Lin. "It's a terrific investment, and they won't go broke on it."

Atlanta, Baltimore, Berlin, Chicago, Cleveland, Detroit, Los Angeles, Minnesota, Munich, the Metropolitan Opera, San Francisco, and Seattle, among many others.

But take care with the phrasing; just because a violinist *owns* a certain instrument may not mean that he or she regularly *plays* it in the orchestra—Bing Wang is a perfect example. And when string players do bring their new instruments to a performance, it may not be for a top-of-the-line program in the concert hall.

While Reuning advocates the use of classic instruments in an orchestra like the Boston Symphony, he also acknowledges that "many BSO players have second instruments [made by contemporary luthiers] that they play in the Boston Pops or for outdoor concerts."

But some players actually take the opposite approach. "Many years ago, when I was playing trumpet in the New York Philharmonic," Gerard Schwarz recalls, "a couple of the string musicians had very good instruments that they left at home, and cheap instruments they played in the orchestra. I thought that was bizarre."

More conventionally, Wang hauls out her Rovatti for plein-air performances and other not-so-special occasions. "I use it for summer outdoor concerts, and sometimes when I have to travel, and sometimes when I have the Guadagnini in the repair shop," she says.

But Wang also points out that a lot of rank-and-file musicians simply don't have the option of using an old Cremonese beauty. "For a lot of students and young players," she says, "a contemporary instrument would be their first violin, and probably their only violin for a long time."

Modern instruments are about the only choice for musicians in regional orchestras. The players aren't paid enough to buy an instrument that costs more than the average board member's house, and the small orchestras' budgets can't accommodate a purchase-and-loan program of the sort that benefits players like Wang.

And then there are those high insurance premiums, which can prove prohibitive for owners of vintage violins. A different sort of generosity, in fact, works against the presence of valuable old instruments in regional orchestras. "I experienced almost a reverse of that [antimodern] bias when I played in Nashville," says Betsy Furth, a cellist in the Nashville Symphony from 1979 to 1997 and now the media and public relations manager of the Aspen Music Festival and School. "Insurance premiums are more expensive for the more valuable instruments and bows [her cello is French, c. 1780], making it harder for an orchestra to afford to cover its players' equipment."

Still, Jan Wilson, the American Symphony Orchestra League's information resource manager, reports, "I do know that many orchestras 'pony up' for instrument insurance—mostly those owned by the orchestra rather than individual musician policies."

Yet several orchestras, such as those of Nashville and Charlotte, North Carolina, have been known to pick up the premiums on instruments owned by the musicians.

CASE OF THE MUTANT VIOLA

If any musician were to get into trouble for playing a new instrument, it would be Don Ehrlich, the San Francisco Symphony's assistant principal violist. He plays a David Rivinus "Pellegrina" ergonomic viola, which looks like a terrestrial instrument cross-bred with extraterrestrial DNA. Among other innovations, it bulges dramatically on the diagonal; sets the neck, bridge, and tailpiece off-center; banks the fingerboard five degrees; and includes extra sound holes.

It's perfect bait for unwanted attention from an ultratraditionalist conductor.

But Ehrlich didn't buy it to goad the guy on the podium; the Pellegrina is the only thing that helped him get over his tendinitis. "Musicians don't mind standing out for their performances, but they hate standing out for anything else," he says. "And here I am with this instrument that is the most notable in the string section; the shape is so odd, and the color is bright, so it draws attention to itself."

Ehrlich set himself up as an irresistible target with his Pellegrina. But he reports that he hasn't experienced open hostility, either from his fellow players or from conductors. "Among my colleagues in the viola section, there is very little enthusiasm for playing something like this themselves, but most don't mind my playing it," he says. "A couple of my colleagues don't like that I play it because of its appearance."

And the response from the podium?

"Mr. [Edo] de Waart took one look at it and said, 'I thought it was my jet lag, and you're not helping,'" Ehrlich recalls. Conductor Laureate Herbert Blomstedt expressed friendly interest in the instrument during a rehearsal break. His successor, Michael Tilson-Thomas, "hasn't said anything directly to me," says Ehrlich, but in the *New York Times* in 1997 the conductor said, "Up to now, we've just been pushing the players. Now we're pushing the instruments."

The *Times* reported that Tilson-Thomas "offered no objection" to Ehrlich's viola.

A QUESTION OF QUALITY?

Still, contemporary instruments do face a lingering, if mild, prejudice. "I think basically that any good conductor is very much concerned about the quality of sound that's coming out of the instruments," says Reuning, "and there's a broad range of quality. There's a small percentage of contemporary instruments that are wonderful sounding, and a large percentage that are not adequate. The vast majority of modern instruments are well below the standard in the field."

Assuming this is true—and it could be debated—even if you do bring a modern instrument into a large, first-rate orchestra, can anyone hear the difference?

"It's hard for me to tell because we only have a few in our orchestra," comments the LA Philharmonic's Wang, "but I don't think it affects the sound, from what I hear. It would be different if we had 10 or 15 of them. For a section to have a beautiful sound quality, your violin should be able to blend with the other violins around you. Some modern instruments have a quieter or a harsher quality, and that makes it hard for you to blend in a sea of older, seasoned instruments."

By the time the sound fills the hall, few audience members could probably detect a mix of old and new. But what about the sharpest ears, positioned right up in front of the orchestra? Aside from Schwarz, the conductors aren't talking, but certain front-rank string soloists aren't shy about expressing an opinion.

Cellist Mischa Maisky definitely prefers to be backed by an orchestra of old instruments. "It's not just a question that modern makers aren't talented enough, but it has to do with the quality of wood and the way it was prepared for the old makers by the generations of families that worked in this profession, and many other processes that very few people understand today," he says. "The fact remains that these old Italian instruments are beyond comparison."

Virtuoso violinist Jaime Laredo is less adamant about the effect old instruments have on players. "You can tell the difference," says Laredo, not too busy as president of the jury of the sixth International Violin Competition of Indianapolis to comment on the subject. "But it's not necessarily the fact that they're all playing on Stradivari violins. It's more the violinist, the violist, the cellist, it's the sound they produce. I believe a first-class player will produce the same great sound on a modern instrument that they will on an old instrument."

Cho-Liang Lin, another well-traveled soloist and Indianapolis judge, agrees. "Eventually this prejudice will have to leave," he says. "It's impossible to insist that only old instruments sound good. Face it—there were plenty of mediocre instruments made 200 years ago, and being 200 years old doesn't make them any better now."

A version of this chapter originally appeared in the April 2003 issue of Strings *magazine.*

CHAPTER 17

13 Steps
to Cello Bliss

How to shop for an instrument priced under $5,000

BY HEATHER K. SCOTT

G reat job!" your teacher exclaims at a recent lesson. "Your tone has really improved, but I think that old rental is beginning to hold you back. Time for us to talk about buying a step-up instrument." Indeed, that old beat-up, but nice-sounding rental from a local dealer has served you well—but now your skills as a player are beginning to develop and your teacher senses that you've become a serious student. It is time for an upgrade. After a couple weeks of research and a handful of phone calls back and forth to your teacher, you set off to visit several dealers in search of a cello equal to your needs. But after your first shop visit, you find yourself feeling woefully overwhelmed and still underprepared for the daunting task of selecting a step-up instrument.

Adult beginners and younger students alike face a unique set of dilemmas when shopping for an instrument, especially if they do so without the advice and experience of a seasoned player. Instrument setup can make or break even the best cello, and knowing what to look for and what will best suit your needs is not as easy as it sounds. Additionally, budget constraints, teachers who suggest only particular brands (be sure to read the *Strings* article on teacher commissions, "An Elegy for Ethics?" in the online *Strings* archives at www.stringsmagazine.com), and not knowing what the market has to offer or how to best evaluate instruments can contribute to the difficulty beginners face when shopping for that first step-up cello.

But don't despair. You can find a decent step-up instrument for between $895 and $5,000. First you'll need a primer in craftsmanship and some tips on how to shop and what to look for. Armed with this knowledge, you should be able to walk into any shop in the world and identify the best cello in your price range.

IT'S ALL IN THE WOOD

Contrary to the old adage "You can't judge a book by its cover," you can often judge an instrument by its appearance. When viewing cellos at your local violin shop, you will instinctively reach for a rich, warm-colored cello with just the right amount of varnish, beautiful flaming, and gorgeous grain rather than a lacquer-finished, candy-apple-red instrument.

Beautiful varnish is not merely aesthetically pleasing. The quality of a cello's varnish will, in fact, affect how an instrument sounds and how that sound will change and mature over the years. Heavily applied varnish can prevent an instrument from "opening up" sonically and cause it to resonate less and less as you play.

Most players don't agree on what color of varnish is best (walnut, chocolate, blond, reddish-orange, and so on). But they do generally agree on how much varnish should be applied to an instrument: most believe that less is best. As Sandy Walsh-Wilson of the Alexander String Quartet says, "I don't want [my] instrument to be weighed down by varnish."

Quality of wood is an important factor in choosing an instrument. Look for instruments made with spruce tops and maple ribs and bottoms. Lesser-quality laminated wood, although durable, is not conducive for good sound (you can spot a laminated cello by looking at the edges of the f-holes, which will reveal the layered cross section). "There are several indicators to help you judge the relative quality of stringed instruments," says Greg Schoeneck, national sales manager for stringed instruments at Conn-Selmer, Inc. (adjuster and finisher of William Lewis & Son, Glaesel, and Scherl & Roth stringed instruments). "Perhaps the easiest to see is the 'flame'. This is the horizontal bar of contrasting light and dark under the varnish in the wood itself. Generally, the more densely flamed the back, sides, and neck are, the more expensive the wood."

Schoeneck adds that buyers should avoid instruments in which the flame has been artificially created. "Real flame is iridescent," he says, "The dark bars become light and the light become dark as the instrument is moved."

A cello's grain will also affect how the instrument performs. A cello's spruce top should have tight grain at its center, under the fingerboard and bridge, growing gradually wider and wider as it reaches out toward the bouts.

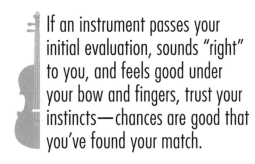

If an instrument passes your initial evaluation, sounds "right" to you, and feels good under your bow and fingers, trust your instincts—chances are good that you've found your match.

Note the quality of the ebony. Schoeneck explains, "Better grades of ebony have tighter grain; the very best being so close-grained that it may appear to be perfectly smooth."

Also "avoid something painted," adds cellist, teacher, and *Strings* contributor Sarah Freiberg. "Is the fingerboard made from real ebony—it should be! Otherwise the wood is likely to be softer, and won't last as long. Also, the paint starts to wear away."

As you look over any cello, check the surface for excessive wear, cracks, or breaks. Your instrument and its wood should be in playing condition—free of any problems that can worsen over time or with prolonged playing. Are the bouts in good condition? There shouldn't be any cracks or chips, either of which can spell disaster later.

"Other things to look for include real, inlayed purfling," recommends Freiberg. Purfling is the inlaid decoration around the top, and sometimes back, edges of an instrument. "Real purfling prevents cracks. It's true that some great makers cheated and painted the purfling on, but the real thing keeps the cello from cracking when it gets inadvertently knocked at the edges."

STAND-UP SETUP

A poorly set up cello, no matter how well it was made, can sound more like a screeching cat than a strong, deep, resonant bass voice with a bright, but not tinny, upper register. Everything from choice of strings to tail-gut material and placement to peg fit influences a cello's playability and performance. "Mechanics are so important," explains Walsh-Wilson. Besides sounding terrible, poor setup can render a potentially good-sounding instrument unplayable. Simply replacing a poorly fit soundpost, cutting a new bridge, adjusting the fittings, or trying out different strings can vastly improve an instrument that might have previously sounded less than desirable.

Does the bridge fit correctly? Look at how the feet sit against the top of the cello; they should exactly fit the belly of the instrument, with the thickness of the feet measuring about 2 mm thick (about the thickness of three credit cards; one credit card measures .7 to .8 mm). The bridge should stand straight with just a slight curve when you look at it from the side (the flat side of the bridge faces the tailpiece and should form a right angle with the top of the cello if viewed from the bass side). Good-quality bridges are generally made out of dense maple, close grained, and highly flamed. Also, note how the strings fit the grooves in the bridge. (Each groove should be properly spaced and deep enough to hold the string securely, but not so deep as to impair the vibration of the string.)

Do the fingerboard and neck feel and look smooth? As you play, feel around the fingerboard for bubbles and dimples in the wood (especially along the long joint between the fingerboard and the neck). A good dealer will make sure that the fingerboard is properly planed and free from any imperfections. You can check this easily by looking closely at the fingerboard: while seated as if playing, position your instrument so that the scroll is even with your chin; in good light, look down the fingerboard—the light should play evenly across the curves of the fingerboard. Another important factor is the long, shallow dip, or scoop, in a properly planed fingerboard. Depress the string at the nut end and at the bridge end of the fingerboard and you can see the scoop at the midpoint of the string. The distance between the string and the fingerboard should be about .9 mm on the treble side and 1 mm–1.4 mm (about two credit cards) on the bass side.

While checking the fingerboard, also observe the neck—it should also be straight, smooth, and without bumps or pits (a good neck will not be varnished, but instead treated with an oil finish).

Are the strings well-suited to the instrument, or are they a one-size-fits-all solution? If you feel that the strings are impeding the sound of the instrument, be sure to ask your dealer if you can try a different set.

Do the fittings match the instrument? More importantly, do they work? Fancy fittings do not a good instrument make and poor fittings can ruin the playability of any instrument. On some instruments, fancy pegs, endpins, or tailpieces can be a sign of a dealer trying to pass off a lesser-quality instrument on an unsuspecting buyer.

Pegs should turn easily and stay in tune (pegs that are too tight or too loose are a sign of improper setup). Also, check that the peg ends are flush with the scroll head—they should not extend out from the scroll, and should indent only slightly into the peg box.

Is the endpin firmly set and does it retract properly? Does the length suit your needs? (Endpins come in either 18-inch or 20-inch sizes, and in a variety of metals.) An endpin that completely disengages from its plug can be an advantage, according to cello maker Peter Van Arsdale. "This gives you the option of changing it out," he says. Does the endpin feel too heavy? Many dealers now offer carbon-fiber endpins. These lighter options, some weighing as little as five ounces, are becoming increasingly popular (although the jury is still out on whether or how they alter the sound of the cello). Endpin prices vary from as little as $40 to as much as $185 and higher.

Note the tailpiece—is it the correct size for the instrument? Does it have built-in fine tuners? (Built-in fine tuners are preferable because they are lighter than tuners you would install and they maintain the proper proportion of string length in front of and behind the bridge.) Is the tailpiece made of plastic, ebony, or composite materials? (Plastic won't resound as nicely as ebony or composite materials when you lightly wrap it with a knuckle.)

Take a peek through an f-hole and look at the soundpost. This small dowel of wood should have no visible cracks or splinters. And it should be positioned about a finger's width from the bridge and behind the right bridge foot. It should also not be leaning, nor should it dimple the top of the cello—you should be able to see this from the outside. (Also, it shouldn't distort the shape of the f-hole.)

THE PRICE IS RIGHT

Before settling in for a test drive with your favorite cellos, you'll need to take a look at those price tags—for some cellists, this is the least favorite part of shopping. Cellos can be expensive, and if your favorite prospect needs additional setup work, that final cost can add up quickly. So plan accordingly.

Before getting out your checkbook, check to see if the cello's price tag matches its aesthetics and craftsmanship, setup, and playability. Does the instrument require more setup in addition to the purchase price? Will the dealer include the setup work in the price or is there an additional fee?

You should also check to see if the dealer accepts trade-ins. If so, in the future you will be able to upgrade the cello for a new one more suited to your growing skill level and needs.

THE TEST DRIVE

It's finally time to sit down and play the cellos that have passed your assessment test, fit within your budget, and spark your interest. Many dealers offer a quiet practice room for playing instruments. Most dealers will let you take your favorite cello home for a test drive.

If you are able to arrange a take-home trial period, be sure to audition your instrument not just at home, but at school, at orchestra rehearsal, in lessons, and wherever else you perform. Instruments will sound different in different venues, and being able to evaluate how your instrument responds—and blends—in small practice rooms, larger rehearsal rooms with other players (in either a chamber or orchestral setting), and in performance halls can influence your final decision.

Enlist the help of a parent, teacher, musician, or friend to listen as you play. Celtic cellist and teacher Natalie Haas suggests, "Get as many other people as you can to listen to you playing this new instrument."

An unbiased teacher can be an important asset as you go through this selection process, as pointed out by Rebecca Ensley, instrument and shop manager for the past 13 years at Southwest Strings (a company that offers a wide range of cellos under $5,000).

"When choosing an instrument as a beginner (or even as an advanced musician), it's always good to seek the advice of a qualified teacher. A good teacher will have some knowledge of makers' names and reputations in the music industry. Ask the teacher to both play and listen to someone else play the potential instrument."

As you play, keep two important factors in mind: tone and playability. Your instrument should not only sound good under your ear, but also across the room—or even at the back of a concert hall. Tone and volume should be even across all strings and in all registers. Choosing a cello is a subjective, gut-feeling endeavor. If an instrument passes your initial evaluation, sounds "right" to you, and feels good under your bow and fingers, trust your instincts—chances are good that you've found your match.

TONE

"Tone is definitely the most important factor [when buying an instrument], but it has to feel good, too," Haas says.

So, how exactly do you test an instrument's tone? First, choose one passage from a piece you're comfortable with and know well—particularly an excerpt that utilizes all strings and multiple playing positions. Listen to the instrument's volume and projection as you play. Is it able to maintain a wide dynamic range, in lower and higher registers, and in first and upper positions? Does it sound good both under the ear and to an audience?

A cello with good tone will project well and cover a wide dynamic range, from the softest pianissimo to the loudest fortissimo, in a clear, distinct voice. Bass instruments can sometimes sound muddy in the lower registers, so be sure to listen for articulation as you play the C and G strings. As you observe tone, especially on the C string, also check the response. The lower, heavier strings should elicit the sound you want—both in volume and in timbre. If you have to work too hard, put down the instrument and move on to another.

Evaluate the tone across all four strings. Does the cello maintain an even sound and tone in the lower, middle, and upper registers? Does the sound hold up as you play in upper positions closer to the bridge?

Check for wolf tones—a possible sign of a good-quality cello. The same resonances necessary to make a good-sounding instrument increase the likelihood of a wolf.

Instrument maker Chris Dungey describes the wolf as "a result of the instability between the vibration of the body of the cello and the vibration of the affected string, which then serve to cancel each other out. The note has barely begun to sound when it disappears. This is repeated again and again and results in the stuttering sound so often heard.

"The wolf note is therefore not the result of a basic structural failure, a faulty repair job, or a misplaced sound post, but, rather, it is an intrinsic characteristic of the instrument. Every properly proportioned cello has a wolf note."

But be aware of how prominent the wolf tones are—if you find them too overpowering, ask your dealer to install a wolf eliminator and give the instrument a second try. If you play the instrument with a wolf eliminator, listen with care—eliminators can also mute other, desirable harmonics.

Finally, does the instrument feel muffled? Does it take little or much effort to elicit decent tone and volume?

PLAYABILITY

In addition to sounding good, your instrument should be comfortable to play. Under your command, it should vary smoothly in volume, tone, and pitch. Notes should be where you'd expect them, pegs and tuners should work and hold tune well, and the instrument as a whole should feel comfortable and responsive under your fingers and bow.

Are the strings responsive and is the action comfortable? You should be able to depress notes smoothly and easily, without much effort—and definitely without feeling like the string is "cutting" into your fingertips. The cello should speak easily, and you should be able to elicit equally loud or soft volume in first position as well as higher positions closer to the bridge.

Equally important, the strings should be spaced properly, allowing each one to vibrate freely without hitting nearby strings.

When looking for a new cello, you want to look for obvious mistakes in the workmanship. Minor flaws on an otherwise good-sounding and comfortable-feeling cello can add character and enhance an instrument. "Yes, even Stradivari made mistakes," says Van Arsdale.

"The difference, however, is that he made them artfully."

While this price bracket is on the lower end of the cello spectrum, you don't have to settle for lesser quality, as Walsh-Wilson points out.

"You can get good instruments in this range," he says.

A version of this chapter originally appeared in the April 2005 issue of Strings *magazine.*

CHAPTER 18

Made in China

The Asian nation has become a major player in the US stringed-instrument market. But consumers must navigate a confusing labyrinth of labels to find the origin of their fiddles

BY KEVIN McKEOUGH

The violins, violas, cellos, and double basses can be found in shops from Berkeley, California, to Des Moines, Iowa, from New York City to Charlotte, North Carolina. They're sold under such names as Andreas Eastman, Johannes Köhr, Andrew Schroetter, and countless others. But no matter how European-sounding their names, many of these shiny new stringed instruments on display in stores throughout the United States share a common origin: China.

Indeed, thousands of stringed instruments on the US market now hail from a country far removed geographically and culturally from the European tradition of string music, and this Asian nation has become a major lutherie center.

As recently as five years ago, there was little love for Chinese-made violins among American instrument buyers and sellers. Since then, however, those instruments have taken the market by storm—especially at the introductory student level—thanks to a combination of improvements in quality and low prices made possible by cheap labor costs.

Yet it's impossible to say how many workshops and factories in China are making and manufacturing stringed instruments. "I've been to dozens of them, and I don't think I've even scratched the surface," reports Stephen Sheppard, president and owner of Tucson, Arizona-based retailer Southwest Strings. "It's a big country."

WHAT'S IN A NAME?

Like many domestic manufacturers, distributors, and retailers, Southwest Strings has become an active partner with the Chinese violin industry, selling both factory-produced instruments under the Klaus Mueller label and workshop-made instruments in the Yuan Qin line.

Even the stores that carry these instruments don't always know who has made them. "We don't know where the workshop is unless our suppliers tell us," explains Matt Zeller, an apprentice violin maker at Donley Violins in Charlotte, North Carolina. "We have suppliers who have family-owned workshops and others who will deal with anyone."

That confusion is widespread. "It's laughable how much rebranding and mismatching and criss-crossing is going on," adds Jason Torreano, product manager for the string brand of the Music Group (formerly Boosey & Hawkes Musical Instruments), which sells its Chinese instruments under the Andrew Schroetter brand. "I wouldn't be surprised if [a single] instrument workshop in China was producing instruments that in the US are being sold under ten or 20 names."

In fact, the import and sale of Chinese stringed instruments has become so widespread that there's literally no way to tell all the names under which they're being sold here. Many of the instruments come to the United States unlabeled, and wholesalers and individual shops attach labels to them that give no suggestion of their provenance. "They'll take an Italian-sounding last name and stick a first name on it, like Medici Alfredo," Zeller observes.

By some estimates, Chinese instruments now hold between 50 and 80 percent of the market for novice violinists.

"Different shops do varying levels of additions," Torreano elaborates. "Some will buy instruments in the white and then do varnish and setups. Others will regradute tops, put in the bass bar. Others are buying them completely made and just putting in a label and adding strings. Once they put their own shop label on it, you won't be able to track a lot of Chinese instruments, because at a certain point they lose their original identity."

To complicate the question of instrument origin further, violin makers in other countries also are importing Chinese-made instrument bodies in the white and finishing them in their shops. This practice allows luthiers in Germany, for example, to claim that the instruments are German-made, since 40 percent of the work (the legal minimum) is performed there.

For consumers and dealers intent on identifying the origin of their instrument, the profusion—and confusion—of names and labels for Chinese-made instruments poses a dilemma. Fortunately, by all accounts the quality of many of these instruments is good, especially by the standards of the beginner level at which they're having the greatest impact.

It wasn't always so.

A DRAMATIC CHANGE

Not long ago, Chinese stringed instruments were maligned as not much better than firewood. The great improvement in their quality is one example of how the advent of a free-market economy and globalism in China has changed both Chinese industry and Western commerce.

In the past, according to Sheppard, Chinese instrument making was done under the control of the Communist Party, which put political bosses in charge of manufacturing. "The bosses didn't know anything about violin making," he says. "That's why the violins had such poor quality. It didn't matter if you made a good instrument or not. With the recent political reforms, [manufacturing operations] now have to make a profit. Therefore, they need to let the free-enterprise system take over, and they have to make good-quality instruments."

The results of that change—prompted by a Chinese government edict that all national industries must eliminate graft, switch to a free-market model, and turn a profit by 2003—have proved impressive. "Generally, they're pretty good," Zeller says of the Chinese-made stringed instruments he's seen since the political reforms took effect. "I've got to say I'm impressed with the quality of the instrument you can get at a low price. They've brought the low end of the market way up in quality while still keeping the price at a low point.

"For the beginning student they're the absolute best out there, because you can get a better quality instrument than a European instrument for several hundred dollars."

FINELY CRAFTED

Zeller also admires the overall workmanship of the Chinese instruments he sells, particularly the graduation on the tops and backs and the Strad-model f-hole placement. Although varnishes on instruments below the $600 range tend towards what he calls "shiny lacquer stuff," past that point instruments typically come with a good-quality spirit varnish. The most common problem he encounters is necks set at the wrong angles, which Zeller says is typical of all instrument makers in the lower price range.

And because China is home to some of the planet's last great stands of old-growth forests, the tonewoods used in the instruments also get good reviews both for durability—Zeller admires the tight grain of the spruce tops, the flame of the maple backs, and the warp-free necks on the instruments he's seen—and for sound.

"Tonally, the Chinese woods are usually regarded as providing a warmer, less penetrating sound," says Joel Becktell, former vice president of Eastman Strings, whose Samuel Eastman, Andreas Eastman, and Mark Moreland instrument lines all are handmade in China by expert craftsmen. "The European tonewoods have a reputation of being more brilliantly focused in their sound."

Thanks to this improved workmanship and the availability of high-quality hardwoods, there is an abundance of excellent Chinese violins, violas, cellos, and double basses available in the United States. In particular, many of the people interviewed singled out the instruments made in China under the supervision of renowned California luthier Scott Cao for praise. The Johannes Köhr line of instruments produced by Alabama's Howard Core Company is also highly regarded by industry peers.

On the other hand, observers also warn that China continues to be a source of some terrible violins, particularly the low-price models sold over the Internet. "When you get down to the $200 ones, there should be a law against selling those things," complains Bill McClain of Atlanta Street Violins in Roswell, Georgia. "They're just selling objects, not real instruments."

He says many of these cheap Chinese violins come with warped fingerboards and poorly fitted bridges and soundposts.

"The setup on them is so horrible that they're virtually unplayable," concurs Richard Ward of Ifshin Violins in Berkeley, California. "The bridges are not even fitted, they're just thrown out there." Ifshin sells its highly regarded Jay Haide line of stringed instruments, which are handmade in Chinese workshops but set up in the States.

Ward also warns of Chinese instrument makers who cut corners during construction by leaving out interior parts, or who use painted white wood, which wears out quickly, instead of ebony or rosewood for the fingerboard and pegs.

> The import and sale of Chinese stringed instruments has become so widespread that there's literally no way to tell all the names under which they're being sold here.

Consumers must rely on retailers to steer them toward the better instruments because of this variance in quality, the difficulty of distinguishing between good and bad violins by name, and the fact that most Chinese instruments are made and priced for student players (or their parents) who have no knowledge of what to look for in an instrument. "You have to be sure you're at a reputable shop that knows what they're doing," Matt Zeller recommends. "You get a lot of people on the Internet who are really just selling trash."

Despite the presence of junk instruments, many Chinese-made student-level violins offer exceptional value at relatively inexpensive prices, which generally range from about $400 to $800 at the retail level (although they can go much higher and lower). As a result, they've quickly taken over a commanding share of the market for new string-music students. By some estimates, Chinese instruments now hold between 50 and 80 percent of the market for novice violinists.

What's all the more remarkable about this market penetration is how quickly it happened. "About three years ago was when it really started to take off," says Alex Weidner, managing partner of the Howard Core Company. "You go back five years, and if you came in with a Chinese violin, people were really skeptical. It has been a dramatic change."

CHINA VS. EUROPE

That change has come largely at the expense of European violin manufacturers, whose labor costs prevent them from competing with Chinese instruments on price and whose reliance on machine manufacturing now sometimes leaves them behind in quality as well. Michael Becker, co-owner of Becker Fine Stringed Instruments in Des Moines (which sells Eastman Strings violins), recalls that for years the standby instruments for beginners came from such manufacturers as Glaesel, Knilling, and Scherl & Roth. "Those were the names that you ran into constantly for entry-level students, and I think the Chinese instruments have given those instruments competition.

"Today, young players have infinitely more options than I had," adds Becker, who in addition to running his music store is a teacher, chamber musician, and violinist for the Des Moines Symphony.

Yet, European violin makers still reign supreme at the higher levels of the violin market. "You don't find [many] high-class instruments [in China], with few exceptions, and those few exceptions will have difficulty being recognized as such," says master violin maker and dealer Fritz Reuter, owner of Fritz Reuter & Sons in Lincolnwood, Illinois, who sells the Snow line of Chinese workshop violins.

For students who have reached the intermediate to advanced level, let alone professionals, the attention to detail found in European and American hand-crafted violins makes them the instruments of choice. "You've got the experienced makers making the high-quality product," acknowledges Weidner. "They've been doing it for generations. To make a superb instrument, they've got the knowledge. To make a student-quality instrument, you can train some workers [to accomplish the task with minimal skills]. To get the detail you need as you move up the ladder, experience is needed."

Pockets of resistance to Chinese instruments still remain on the student level, as well. In some cases, schools have had such bad luck with inferior Chinese instruments in the past that they have discouraged their students from renting them. In others, cultural biases remain an obstacle. "Some people will always want a European instrument, they'll always want a German violin," notes H. R. Core, marketing manager for Howard Core Company.

For the most part, though, acceptance of Chinese-made instruments has been growing steadily, a trend that not only is affecting violin manufacturing and sales, but also is having beneficial effects on an entire generation of aspiring string musicians. There's little doubt that over the long run the increasing accessibility and affordability of higher-quality Chinese instruments will benefit buyers and sellers alike.

"Because there are so many inexpensive instruments out there," Jason Torreano says, "the number of kids who are starting on stringed instruments is multiplying."

A version of this chapter originally appeared in the October 2003 issue of Strings *magazine.*

CHAPTER 19

It's a Small World

Finding the right-size fractional instrument
requires a good ear for tone

BY RICHARD WARD

I n spite of chronic loss of funding for our schools and the subsequent elimination of music programs, it seems as if more young children than ever are playing stringed instruments. It also seems that parents are starting their children on music lessons at a younger age and often want them to benefit from the advantage of a good-quality instrument. These parents realize that violin-family instruments are not the easiest to learn, and the disadvantage of a poorly made instrument is a real handicap.

Stringed instruments have always been made in a variety of sizes, from the standard full-size (referred to as 4/4) down to violins as small as 1/32, which might be used by a two- or three-year-old child. These sizes are always expressed in fractions, hence the term "fractional sizes" when talking about these small stringed instruments. However, that doesn't mean that a 3/4-size is three-quarters the size of a full-size (4/4) violin. If it did, a 3/4 violin would be four inches shorter. In reality, a 3/4 size violin has a body length one inch shorter than a full-size. These so-called fractions are simply a convenient system that has been developed to indicate the different sizes. There is roughly a one-inch difference in size between each of the quarter sizes. A 7/8-size violin is about a half inch smaller than a 4/4. This is true of violins, cellos, and basses. With violas, size is expressed in actual body length. A standard full-size viola is 16 inches, and anything under 15 inches is considered below standard size.

SOUND ADVICE

The trick to searching for a small stringed instrument is finding one with the best possible sound. Because of their reduced size, these smaller instruments have a weaker, somewhat one-dimensional sound that lacks the fullness and depth of the standard-size instruments.

The smaller the size, the weaker the sound, all other things being equal.

Lauren Elledge, a colleague, started playing the viola when she was eight on a 1/4 violin strung with viola strings. She still remembers how awful the sound was, especially on the lower strings. Yet, a well-made and adjusted 3/4- or even 1/2-size violin can sound almost as good as a full-size, but the smaller ones never will. While there are tonal compromises one must accept, you can find a good, playable small instrument.

For the beginning student, I recommend a good rental from a shop that specializes in stringed instruments, rather than a purchase. That way, if the child

---

∽ SIZING UP YOUR PLAYER ∽

On the average, a child will stay in a given fractional size for about two years. Normally you should trust the teacher to let you know what the appropriate size should be. When you change instrument size, you may need to change the bow size as well, unless the student's arms are unusually long or short.

There is a bit of confusion about some of the actual sizes. Most ¾ violins are similar in size, with a body length of about 13 inches to 13¼ inches; ½-size instruments have a wider range. There is a "Suzuki size" that is smaller than the "German Size" and can vary by as much as a half inch in body length. There are similar variations in the ¼ violins as well.

Always use strings appropriate to the instrument. The string size should match the instrument. Fractional-size strings aren't just shorter versions of the corresponding full size. They are usually a bit thicker, increasing the tension and improving the sound. If you use a string intended for a larger-size instrument, the strings will probably break more easily.

If you want your young student to enjoy learning to play his or her stringed instrument, get the best one possible within your budget, preferably from a violin specialist. This will go a long way toward helping your budding young Joshua Bell or Hilary Hahn.

—R.W.

FRACTIONAL SIZE CHART (IN MM)

	4/4	3/4	1/2	1/4	1/8	1/16
Body* length	356	335	310	280	255	230
Total length	590	550	520	462	419	n/a
String length	325	310	285	260	235	215
Player size ** inches	23 5/8+	22 1/4–23 5/8	20 1/4–22 1/4	18 1/2–20 1/4	16 7/8–18 1/2	14–15 1/4

CELLO	4/4	3/4	1/2	1/4
Body* length	755	690	650	580
Total length	1,240	1,130	1,060	952
String length	680	635	600	535
Player size ** inches	23 5/8+	22 1/4–23 5/8	20 1/4–22 1/4	18 1/2–20 1/4

  * Body length is the length of the back less the button at the top of the back.
 ** Measure the distance from the neck to the center of the palm with the arm stretched out straight.

loses interest, the instrument can be returned with only a minimal investment. After a year or two, you can usually tell if a child will stick with it. Then, purchasing the fractional instrument starts to make sense. After a year or so of renting, a good shop should give you some sort of credit toward purchase. If you do purchase, make sure you can trade the instrument in when the child grows into the next size. You don't want to be left with an instrument you can't easily sell. Sometimes you can purchase something from the family of a student who has outgrown it. Just make sure that the price is fair and that the instrument is in good condition. At some point, you will have to sell it.

You don't want to end up with a house full of small-size violins.

LIMITED CHOICE

There are plenty of interesting-sounding full-size instruments out there for sale. The situation with smaller sizes is a bit different, with new and 20- to 30-year-old instruments dominating the market. In the past, makers were reluctant to make good-quality small instruments for what they viewed as a limited market.

Today, with the growth in demand for good smaller instruments, violin makers are starting to produce better 3/4- and 1/2-size instruments. I've played on some

A well-made and adjusted 3/4- or even 1/2-size violin can sound almost as good as a full-size.

3/4 violins and even 1/2-size violins that sounded remarkably like a full-size instrument. If you want a good older instrument, you may need to spend more time in your search.

The European masters of the 18th and early 19th centuries occasionally made instruments on order for a specific client, but these are rare. Some of the German or French commercial makers of the late 19th and early 20th centuries made fractional sizes, but normally in their least expensive models.

I have found some 60- to 100-year-old French instruments from the Mirecourt workshops of Marc Laberte and Thibouville-Lamy that, if well set up, can be very good. There are also good vintage fractional-size instruments from the German workshops. However, I've never seen small instruments from the big Markneukirchen workshops of Ernst Heinrich Roth or Heinrich Heberlein.

Overall, the supply of quality vintage fractional instruments continues to diminish. Children can be careless and many of these small fiddles have not survived. While musicians have traditionally preferred older instruments, you may find that a good-quality new fractional sounds as good as, or sometimes even better than, something old.

A version of this chapter originally appeared in the February 2007 issue of Strings *magazine.*

CHAPTER 20

Patience and Band-Aids

A beginner's guide to building a stringed-instrument kit

BY HEATHER K. SCOTT

t was a breezy but unseasonably warm February day in the San Francisco Bay Area. I was outside on my deck, now one-half hour into filing a small piece of wood into four separate and much smaller pieces. Yes, filing, not sawing: the small power saw that I'd just attempted to use (rather naively) elicited disastrous results, splintering my wood to bits; the small handsaw I'd tried next was woefully dull (note Band-Aid on thumb). And now, losing my patience and feeling desperate, I coaxed an old, metal file through the groove I'd started in a final attempt to finish the cut.

Growing impatient, I exerted more pressure. The file jumped its furrow, snagging the knuckle of my yet-to-be-bandaged thumb, eliciting words I best not quote here.

This was my first day of work on a viola kit I'd purchased nearly four months prior. I'd been nervous to start construction and had finally steeled myself to begin my assignment. Earlier that week, I'd met with my mentor, luthier Haide Lin at Ifshin Violins in Berkeley, California, feeling positive and prepared. I'd spent the past four months studying *The Art of Violin Making*, by Chris Johnson and Roy Courtnall, as if I were cramming for a college final, and until I'd clamped my block of wood into its orange vice, wielded my saw, and begun work, I hadn't realized how unprepared I was.

All that textbook knowledge soon disappeared, falling to pieces like the wood shavings and splinters now collecting at my feet. My first lutherie lesson turned out to be less about cutting blocks and more about tools and patience.

A few years ago, I was fortunate enough to visit with several makers in Eastern Europe. Entering those shops filled with the hearty smell of wood and the astringent bite of varnish, and watching master makers work so deftly and devotedly on their crafts made a lasting impression. Shortly after returning to the States, I ordered a kit, curious to see if I had what it takes to build a viola.

For musicians interested in learning the technical ins and outs of bowed stringed instruments, a kit can provide an incredible opportunity to get to know your instrument from the inside out. And for those determined souls who actually finish, these instruments can become a lovely conversation piece—or even a decent axe. The trade market offers a variety of instrument kits. From raw tonewood to instruments in the white, you can begin your lutherie quest at just about any skill level.

CHOOSING A KIT

How do you know if kit building is right for you—or what kit is best for your ability? You'll need to consider how much time, realistically, you can devote to the job, what type of kit you can afford, if you have woodworking experience, if you want to buy tools and/or have time to learn how to use them, and what your primary goals are. "If you get satisfaction from the creative process, and have the basic skills needed, kits are a wonderful idea," says Bill Taylor, owner of Lark in the Morning, an instrument dealer with shops in San Francisco, Mendocino, and Seattle (www.larkinthemorning.com). "But, if you're just trying to save money on a finished instrument, it's probably not a great idea. There are many well-built stringed instruments (violins, guitars, cellos, and so on) at very affordable prices, and they compare very well to anything you'd get from a kit."

Admittedly, when I first started my kit, I'd indulged in fantasies of sitting in a community-orchestra rehearsal with a beautifully finished viola, complete with my own maker's label. But, the main reason I'd chosen to tackle kit building was simply to see if I could do it. I looked for a kit with a fair amount of construction— but also one that wouldn't be beyond my scope of completion. Raw wood wasn't for me; nor was an instrument in the white. So, I finally settled on a "piecemeal" kit with both pre-cut and raw materials.

But there are other options to consider. If you're not looking for a full lutherie experience, or just don't have the time or tools, you can opt for an instrument in the white (cut but unvarnished), and focus on just varnish and set up.

If you're like me and you want a healthy mix of finished and raw materials, look for kits that offer partially carved pieces (rough scroll and neck, fittings, fingerboard, and pre-cut top and back). If you have the time and are serious about the learning process, look for workshops or classes that offer kits along with their tuition cost. And if you want the ultimate lutherie experience (but don't want to enroll in a four-year program at a reputable school), seek out kits of raw wood (uncut but prepared tonewood; or raw, dry, round logs).

For a comprehensive list of kits, workshops, and supplies visit the *Strings* Buyer's Guide online at www.stringsmagazine.com.

TOOLS AND COST

One of my favorite early kit experiences was building a small T-square from a scrap of rosewood; I've used this tool in every work session since. Building this handy tool included all of the important first steps for making an instrument: understanding the importance of exact measurements (in lutherie, everything boils down to millimeters), patience, and the importance of finding and using good, sharp tools. For many beginners, building and/or practicing with wood working tools is the best place to start your lutherie experience.

Tools are indeed an essential—and sometimes hidden—part of instrument making. The old adage of using the right tools for the right job is exceedingly apparent in this trade. There is a one-line entry in my work journal, three months into the project, that simply says, "To do: Get the right tools. And make sure they are sharp."

Some of the tools you'll need to complete your instrument kit include: gouges and chisels, knives, purfling tools, files and rasps, saws, scrapers, calipers, planes, clamps, a T-square, and such power tools as a drill press, band saw, power sander, and jig. The best way to discern exactly which tools you will need is to ask when you purchase your kit. When I placed my initial call to Howard Core, the customer service representative read a list of tools that I'd need, in addition to a good bag of hide-glue mix. Nearly all shops and kit suppliers offer this information to customers (or point them towards resources where they can find answers and cost estimates). In many cases, shops and suppliers that sell kits and tonewoods also sell tools.

"We sell several types of gouges and chisels, knives, purfling tools, files and rasps, hole saws for the f-holes, and some other tools," says Edward C. Campbell of Chimney's Violin Shop. You can also contact Atlantic Violin Supplies (www.atlanticviolinsupplies.com), International Luthiers Supply, Inc. (www. internationalluthiers.com), Specialty Violin (www.specialtyviolin.com), and Japan Woodworker (www.japanwoodworker.com) to inquire about tools and what you'll need to finish your kit.

How much can you expect to spend on a kit? For a basic, pre-cut kit, several hundred dollars and just as much, if not more, on tools. "The cost of materials varies quite a lot," says Roman Barnas, a lutherie instructor at the North Bennett Street School. And instrument-kit costs can be difficult to estimate, adds Jeff Cardey, wholesale manager at Geo Heinle & Co., Ltd. It all depends on the level of difficulty you choose, and how many tools you'll need.

For a beginner, you can "get away with using one 12 mm-width plane, a marking caliper or graduating caliper, soundpost setter, peg reamer, peg shaver, two strap clamps and a dozen or so spool clamps—around $200 to $300 worth of tools (these are ballpark figures)," says Rob Juzek of Metropolitan Music Co. in Vermont (www.metmusic.com).

"Materials [in general] will cost between $500 and $600," says Cardey. "But it's the tools that will break the bank," he concurs. "You could get away with a smaller amount of tools to start," he says, but keep in mind the job will take longer.

I spent roughly $250 for my piecemeal kit, and nearly $200 (so far) on additional tools alone (three finger plains, files, and a gouge). I will eventually need to either borrow or invest in some of the more expensive tools—such as calipers. And, finally, I'll need to order varnish.

For the beginner, this is another reason why finding a workshop, class, or mentor can be so helpful. If you can borrow tools, you can greatly decrease your production costs.

WHERE TO BEGIN

The experience of building an instrument, whether it is from a kit or from raw wood, is rife with trials. One such challenge is simply getting started.

As Cardey aptly states, "A job started is half done. It's true. Ask any maker and they'll tell you it's always hardest before you start."

I can vouch for Cardey's statement. I called Howard Core to order my viola kit in November 2003 . . . and didn't start construction until February 2004. For me, a box full of parts, a book, and a handful of basic tools just weren't enough. I needed to find in-depth, step-by-step instructions, in addition to a good book to study. For me, having a solid reference and someone to talk with in person were essential. That person was Haide Lin.

"Many kits do not have detailed instructions, and are designed for someone who already has knowledge, or is comfortable researching the things he or she doesn't know," Taylor says. If you are going to tackle building from a kit, and you don't have a lutherie background, you'll be doing yourself a great disservice to not seek out a shop or maker to mentor you through the process. Some shops and suppliers can offer you help along the way, so be sure to check when you order your kit or your parts.

Chances are if you are an absolute beginner, like me, having a mentor, taking classes, attending a workshop, or seeking out other "green" makers on Web boards will be an integral part of your kit-building success. There are a plethora of online resources, from the forums hosted by Leif Luscombe of Luscombe Violins, Inc. in Ontario, Canada (www.violins.on.ca), to online classes and support, like those found at the Musical Instrument Makers Forum (www.mimf.com). Through these resources, and through the shop or supplier where you purchase your kit, you should be able to find the help you need.

"Making has many challenges; mostly for those unfamiliar with wood working," explains Luscombe. "Those with a background in fine woodworking and using hand tools have a great advantage."

Barnas agrees, saying, "Among more common problems of beginning students is finding patience to learn the basic skills first." He adds, "Safety, tool usage, and tool maintenance are the most important beginning steps for an aspiring instrument maker. Once learned they help to avoid many mistakes and problems in the future."

Patience is key. A beginner is bound to make mistakes, and needs to be prepared for anything—from being able to reglue an opened seam, to having the patience to cut and recut corner blocks, to living with an unfixable gouge in a finished rib (all were mistakes and problems I encountered).

"As with any project, patience is a great asset; most mistakes are made when rushing or applying too much force," says Luscombe. "Beginning makers should mentally work through each process thoroughly to anticipate the various challenges, setup, and tools that will be required at each step of the process. Careful adherence to the measurements and sharp tools are a must," he adds.

Cardey agrees, "An aspiring student of the trade is not only bound to make mistakes, it's guaranteed that mistakes will be made. That is how one truly learns

ᴄ⌣ SOME ASSEMBLY REQUIRED ⌣ᴄ

No matter what your level of interest, or instrument type, there is a stringed-instrument kit on the market that should meet your needs. Take the time to shop around and familiarize yourself with the various types.

DIY Precut and Raw Wood Kits

Several shops, such as Lark in the Morning, located in San Francisco and Mendocino, California, and Seattle, Washington, offer a variety of do-it-yourself kit options. Owner Bill Taylor, reports that his shop sells both domestic and European wood kits. "Our kits vary widely," adds Taylor. "Some are essentially just assembly and finishing, others are much more detailed."

Metropolitan Music Co. added Hofner beginner (pre-cut and partially glued) and advanced (partially cut, not assembled) kits to their catalog. The company also sells a variety of tonewoods. "We like to tell people that they are welcome to stop by our shop to pick out their own wood," says Juzek. "This is really the best way to get exactly what you are looking for. We can help a beginner choose a good piece of wood as well."

Instruments in the White

If you're looking for the most basic violin-making experience, purchasing an instrument in the white is the best choice. Geo Heinle sells these types of ready-made instruments in the white. Jeff Cardey

of Geo Heinle & Co. describes this product as, "a fully assembled violin that has no varnish," and adds that this is a good option if you're looking for more of a varnish focus.

You can also find instruments and kits in the white at Quinn Violins (www.quinnviolins.com), International Violin Co. (www.internationalviolin.com), and Saga Musical instruments (www.sagamusic.com).

Tonewood Kits

Conversely, if you have some woodworking experience, and are looking for the *ultimate* lutherie challenge, look for places where you can purchase raw tonewood and pre-carved parts (or even unfinished parts), and tools to tackle an instrument from scratch. Luscombe also offers a helpful violin making and restoration forum on his website at www.violins.on.ca/forum.

Howard Core wholesale supplier also offers a selection of kit options, from raw wood sold in "wood assortment bags" (premium-quality, round, dry, French boxwood—about as raw as you can get) to the Hofner violin kit (all pre-cut pieces, finished and ready for assembly and varnish—also includes a step-by-step instruction guide for building). Other resources for raw tonewood include Specialty Violins (www.specialtyviolins.com), European Tonewoods (www.europeantonewoods.com), and Rivolta Tonewoods (www.riwoods.com).

> '**We like to tell people that they are welcome to stop by our shop to pick out their own wood.**'
>
> —JOHN JUZEK

in all aspects of life. You make your mistakes so you know what not to do next time around.

"Violin making is a very difficult trade. It requires more patience and attention to detail than most people are willing or even capable of devoting."

Nearly three years after calling Howard Core to make my order for a 16 1/2–inch viola kit, I am still building and equally fascinated and frustrated by this high art. It isn't an easy project; kit building has taught me much more than lutherie skills. I've had to temporarily put my project on hold in the wake of a cross-country move and will start once again when I can partner with a mentor and borrow tools; I look forward to finding a workshop or class through which to finish my kit soon.

The process is one that garners more of my respect today than when it did before I started my kit. Only until you attempt to cut your own bouts (without nicking the corners), bend your own ribs (without burning the wood), and cut blocks (without putting a gash in your thumb), do you really understand a stringed instrument.

"Luthiers are truly a breed of their own," says Cardey, "with a set of skills and knowledge that many can aspire to but few will reach or even begin to comprehend how it is that you take a hunk of wood and create functional beauty that in turn inspires one to make music.

"It truly is a wondrous act."

A version of this chapter originally appeared in the April 2006 issue of Strings *magazine.*

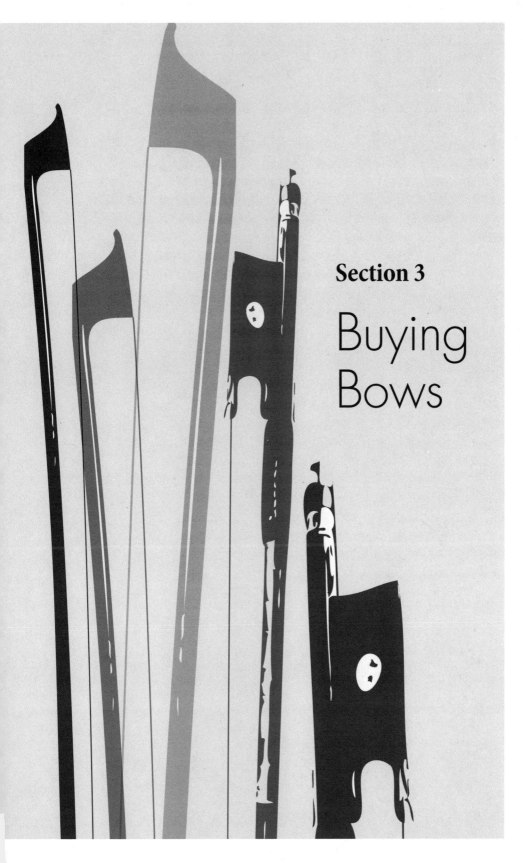

Section 3

Buying
Bows

CHAPTER 21

Best Bow

Finding the right stick for you

BY RICHARD WARD

Choosing a bow can be a daunting task, given the multitude of products on the market. Here are several simple points to consider when, checkbook in hand, you venture off to visit your local dealer in search of the perfect stick to suit your needs.

If you're a beginner with limited technical skills, you make few demands of your bow. It isn't likely that you'll yet need the qualities of a fine and expensive bow. For now, you simply need a bow with a reasonably strong stick and a good camber (curve); a bow that's not too heavy or light and with a proper balance. As your skills increase, however, so do your demands on the bow and hopefully your ability to recognize the differences.

The best way to describe the best bow for any player is simply this: When you are performing, you don't have to think about it. A good bow should become an extension of your right hand. It should flow with you as you play—with little effort or thought. When you pick up a fine French bow—perhaps a Peccatte or a Voirin—or a well-made modern bow, you can instantly feel that the bow has the power to perform better, giving you more confidence and allowing you to play with less effort. So, if you fail in your bowing technique, it's due to your own lack of skill or preparation—and not the bow's fault.

Before you start your quest for a bow, there are a few things you should know about the selection process.

TYPE OF MATERIAL

The three basic materials used in bow sticks are brazilwood, pernambuco, and carbon fiber.

Brazilwood is a generic name given to several kinds of tropical hardwoods used for inexpensive bows. It comes from Brazil as well as other tropical countries. Brazilwood violin bows are normally priced between about $50 and $200 and are suitable for beginning or possibly early intermediate players.

Since the late 18th century, pernambuco has been the wood of choice for the best bows. It's a dense, heavy wood that comes from several areas in Brazil and seems to possess just the right combination of strength, elasticity, and responsiveness. There are many subspecies and enormous variation in quality. Top master bow makers will spend a great deal of time looking for and choosing only the very best pernambuco sticks, rejecting most everything else. Due to environmental degradation, pernambuco is now scarce, and as a result, the government of Brazil has put severe restrictions on the export of this wood, making it rare and expensive.

The lack of available pernambuco may be responsible for the quality of products on the bow market. Many players consider the work of the great 19th-century French makers as the ultimate bows. Why have the later makers not been able to equal their work? Some say that the species of pernambuco used by their predecessors no longer exists and that it became extinct at the beginning of the 20th century. Others feel that makers like Tourte, Peccatte, Simon, Pajot, and their contemporaries were simply the best makers. Certainly their bows are unique. Many have a smooth, supple quality that makes the bow almost part of your hand; the sound these bows produce can be full and rich. More than once, I've heard the phrase "smooth as butter" in describing a fine old French bow. However, other players prefer modern bows that are stiffer, stronger, and quicker in response.

If you don't know much about bows, I suggest you try lots of bows to educate yourself about what is available.

Within the last 20 years, carbon-fiber bows have become popular, in part because of the shortage of pernambuco. Carbon-fiber bows—manufactured from various grades of carbon fiber bonded with a resin—possess many of the qualities of pernambuco. Carbon fiber is also durable, and at its price range represents a good value.

Fiberglass has also been used for inexpensive bows sometimes found with the lowest-priced student instruments. Their main advantage is durability and affordability.

Regardless of the material you select, all bows share certain considerations when it comes to their playability.

SOUND

Inexperienced players are often surprised at how different bows can create different sounds on their instruments. These differences are subtle and can be clearly heard by the player under the ear, but can sometimes be heard by the audience as well. The esteemed American bow maker Morgan Andersen tells us that a suppler bow will have a smoother, fuller sound. However, if the stick is too soft, the sound can lack clarity and definition. A stiffer, stronger bow will give a brighter, more focused sound. Sometimes, an overly stiff bow can produce a rough, edgy sound. It's difficult to find a bow that will give both a smooth broad sound and at the same time have great clarity of focus and the quickness of response that comes from a stronger, stiffer bow.

WEIGHT AND BALANCE

The average weight of a violin bow is about 60 grams (a viola bow is 70 grams; a cello bow, 80 grams). But remember, this is only an average. Many bows by the great makers of the past weigh as little as 54 grams and yet play beautifully. On the other hand, a 66- or 68-gram violin bow would be too heavy for almost anyone. Proper balance is far more important than weight. I know players who won't even look at a bow if it doesn't weigh 60 grams. By holding to this standard, they are missing out on some great bows. If a bow feels right in your hand, it probably is right. I will often pick up a bow and hold it at a 45-degree angle. A bow should feel natural in the hand—well balanced from tip to frog with equal weight throughout.

ROUND OR OCTAGONAL?

The great French master makers rarely made octagonal bows. Even today, most top makers produce predominantly round bows. Yet, as an instrument dealer, I sometimes have players who only want to look at octagonal bows. With two bows made from the same wood, the octagonal shaft will be stiffer. Some octagonal bows are quite stiff, creating a hard, one-dimensional tone, lacking nuance. Some

∽ BOW RATING ∽

"There are three important things to consider in choosing a bow," renowned Parisian bow maker Stéphane Thomachot once told *Strings*: "No. 1 is sound, No. 2 is sound, and No. 3 is sound." The first four characteristics listed in the chart below are the keys to evaluating the potential sound produced by a bow. The remaining items go into more detail, helping you to identify specific factors in producing that sound. Before you shop, take a moment to assess the strengths and weaknesses of your current bow and determine what you want your new bow to accomplish. And remember that no single bow is likely to be ideal for everything (solo work, chamber music, and so on) or to perform well in every environment (the sound qualities of performance spaces vary). So you most likely will need several bows to meet your various needs.

A CHECKLIST FOR RATING BOWS

Suggested rating scale: Poor = 1, Fair = 2, Average = 3, Good = 4, Excellent = 5

ATTRIBUTE	YOUR BOW	TRIAL BOW
1. Strength/overall firmness		
2. Flexibility		
3. Weight		
4. Balance		
5. Stability (no shaking when played)		
6. Firmness (at tip, middle, and frog)		
7. Legato		
8. Staccato		
9. Ricochet		
10. Sautillé		
11. Overall sound quality (piano, forte, and so on)		
12. Ease of playing		
13. Appearance (aesthetic qualities)		
14. Condition (damage or wear)		
15. Value		
16. Other		
TOTAL RATING (add points)		

of the German commercial-bow producers make a round and octagonal version of the same bow, the octagonal being a bit more expensive. I think this has added to the myth that octagonal bows are better.

IN THE SHOP

So how should you go about finding the best bow? The first step is to establish a budget, but do expect to look at bows that are a little more expensive. If you don't know much about bows, I suggest you try lots of bows to educate yourself about what is available.

When you go to a shop, be sure to bring your own violin and current bow with you as a benchmark. Each bow will perform differently on different instruments, so remember that you're looking for a bow that complements your violin. I normally show six bows at a time. Once you've chosen one or two from that batch, ask to see some more. Play the same very brief passage with each bow, one right after another. There's a good chance that one or two will stand out.

First impressions are very important. The bow shouldn't seem too light or heavy in the hand. It shouldn't be too weak or soft: It shouldn't collapse easily on the hair when playing, or flex too much laterally. And it should be straight when viewed down the stick.

Play a combination of bowing styles, including legato, spiccato, sautillé, and so on. When I try bows, I often use Wieniawski's Etudes-Caprices Op. 18, No. 4, to give me an idea of how the bow performs in difficult, rapid string-crossing passages. If that's too difficult, use some of the Ševčik bowing exercises. Play a passage near the frog, in the middle, and near the tip. You should be able to play comfortably with all parts of the bow. Playing slowly, listen to the sound each bow produces and feel how the bow handles. You'll notice subtle differences in clarity, fullness of sound, surface noise, and so on. Does the bow enhance or detract from your instrument?

While you're in the shop, use your time efficiently. You're there to find a bow, not to perform or practice. Once you've picked out the two or three bows you prefer, ask to test them out for a week. Try them more extensively at home, in your ensemble or orchestra, and show them to your teacher for comments. If your teacher's suggestions are important to you, be sure that he or she is available within the week. However, showing the bows to too many other players will only confuse you. Everyone will probably have a different opinion and those opinions may not be helpful.

Remember, the bow will be yours, not theirs. You should make the final decision.

A version of this chapter originally appeared in the March 2004 issue of Strings *magazine.*

CHAPTER 22

Fetching the Stick

The delicate art of commissioning a bow—
and one or two tips on how to do it

BY DAVID TEMPLETON

The modern stringed-instrument bow was more or less perfected in the first half of the 19th century. The basic elements in the construction of any bow— the stick, the frog, the head—are, as Portland, Oregon, bow maker Michael Yeats describes them, "fundamental essentials" that remain constant, having already been fussed over and sorted out by the great bow makers of the 18th and 19th centuries. In other words, a bow is a bow is a bow.

There is only so much a person can do to a bow before it stops being a bow— and becomes something else. Something like a very expensive stick. That said, a modern bow maker with any breadth of experience can easily see, within the constricts of the bow's essential design, a thousand tiny variables that make each bow unique in sound and performance.

Whatever a player's reason for seeking a new bow, an experienced maker has the power to provide something that specifically matches each player's vastly varying desires. So, while some might say that a bow is a bow is a bow, it is also true that in the hands of a skilled maker, a bow can be made to fit an endless number of needs.

"Buying a violin bow is like buying a suit," says bow maker Matt Wehling, who has won four Violin Society of America (VSA) gold medals for his work. "Let's say you're hoping to get one off the rack. If you look long enough, and you have a good enough idea what you want and you can express that pretty well, and if you narrow down all the suit shops in town until you know which ones you can work with, then you can probably buy a suit off the rack that is a pretty good fit.

"But," he adds, "it's never going to fit as well or be as good as the suit you had tailored to your body. It's the same with buying a bow. It's a matter of having something made exactly to fit your needs as opposed to just hoping to find something that sort of happens to meet your needs."

A one-time chemist and former Irish fiddler (he now plays the mandolin), Wehling apprenticed for ten years in France, and runs a thriving bow shop in Northfield, Minnesota, 42 miles south of St. Paul. He has earned a reputation for crafting beautiful bows—the made-to-order kind as well as the off-the-rack variety—and has built an impressive worldwide client roster that includes the members of Kronos Quartet. With his current waiting list, it usually takes Wehling about two months to supply a client with a standard-issue bow, and a bit longer for a commissioned one.

WHERE TO START

Having established that commissioning a bow will usually result in a satisfying match of bow and player, what exactly can a player expect from the process of having a bow tailor-made to his or her needs? And how does one begin the process?

Naturally, you'll need to find a bow maker in the first place. You might start by contacting the VSA at www.vsa.to or the American Federation of Violin and Bow Makers (AFVBM) www.afvbm.com. You'll also find listings for many bow makers in Strings' annual Buyer's Guide, available online at www.stringsmagazine.com.

The process proceeds with a lot of questions, on the part of the player and the maker. "There's a lot of work involved in having a bow made for you," admits Wehling. "You have to know what you want, which is not always the easiest thing, and you have to be able to communicate what you want, which can also be difficult."

When you commission a bow from an experienced maker, long before the actual work begins, you can expect to spend a lot of time discussing music: What music do you play? How do you play your instrument? Do you play solo, in an orchestra, or in a small ensemble? The way you answer such questions will influence the end result. "I recently did a made-to-order bow for a cello player," Wehling recalls, "and she was very specific about the sort of projection she hoped to achieve for her orchestral needs, as opposed to what she expected from her chamber playing. So people need to be very specific about what they want to achieve."

Only then will talk turn toward the physical aspects of the bow itself: Which bows have you played? What did you like about them? What did you hate? Do you want a silver headplate or an ivory headplate? Whalebone, silk, or silver wrap? Gold mounted or silver?

As for the type of wood: Pernambuco is more than the standard, these makers say, it's the only game in town.

The price you pay for a made-to-order bow will vary from maker to maker, based on that maker's experience and reputation, the grade of wood and other materials used, and such requests as gold mounting, gold inlay, or other specific ornamentation. A reasonably new maker might charge $2,000, while a living legend—not hard to find, actually—might charge $5,000 or $6,000 and sometimes more. Wehling's price for a custom silver-mounted bow starts at around $3,800. For a bit extra, he'll stop just short of completing the job and have the buyer come to his shop and play their instrument with the nearly finished bow. Then he'll make whatever changes seem appropriate, either changing the camber or actually taking wood off the stick where needed.

"So," he says, "you truly are getting a tailor-made bow."

GOOD AS OLD?

"Bows are kind of a mystery," says Erin Shrader, a bow maker and restorer formerly with David Stone Violins in Seattle (now *Strings'* lutherie editor). "How they work with each violin is different. And that, absolutely, is why making bows is so much fun. When you rosin it up for the first time, it's always exciting. 'What's it going to sound like?'"

For Shrader—who builds the occasional made-to-order bow, although most of her bows are of the noncommissioned variety—the appeal of a brand new bow lies partly in how it can be created to fit a player's needs and partly in its price compared to the fine old bows many players prefer.

"If you're not hung up on an old bow," says Shrader, "a modern bow is a great value."

She cites the example of a violinist friend whose "lovely old bow was accidentally broken." After looking at some other old bows, the friend discovered she could buy a matched set of exceptional gold-mounted bows, made recently by an award-winning bow maker, for the insurance settlement on her old bow. She made the purchase.

"Not everyone agrees with this," Shrader says, "but I think that the quality of the bows made by top makers today is as good as the bows made by top makers from the turn of the century."

Shrader is right; not everyone agrees.

After 25 years as a bow maker, and with a client list that reads like the *Who's Who* of famous violinists, New York-based bow maker Yung Chin—who does nothing but commissioned bows—has come to believe that the bows of great old makers have a few significant advantages.

"For one thing, the quality of the wood is better in some of the best old bows," he says, "and then, because they are old, the wood has stabilized. The older bows have oils in them, and resins, and it can take years for the bow to season. Even with the bows I made 25 years ago, the sound has changed over time."

But Chin agrees that a major part of the appeal of modern bows is their price. "If your basic modern bow maker gets $2,500 to $4,500 for a silver-mounted bow," he says, "you have to ask yourself, 'What can I get in the old bow market in that kind of price range?' In old French bows, there's nothing. You can't touch anything for that kind of money. So that's an obvious advantage when looking at modern bows, and the others are that, one, you know who actually made it—not always the case with some old bows—and two, a modern maker can give you whatever characteristics you ask for."

With a laugh, Chin admits to having once turned down a commission from a mediocre violinist, partly because of his playing but also because he was a backup musician for New Age megastar Yanni. Yet once he has accepted a commission, Chin says, he usually wants to watch the player in action, always on his or her own instrument, and he gives them a variety of bows to play with.

"It's very important to observe a player with his instrument, because I want to know how he interacts with the bow and the instrument, and I also want to break down the sound of the instrument," he says. "Is it a bright sound, or a dark sound? What is the timbre of the tone? All of those are things that figure into the equation when I make a bow.

"Making a bow for a client is an interesting chess game," he adds, "and it's important—for the maker and the player—to know all the pieces."

A version of this chapter originally appeared in the October 2003 issue of Strings *magazine.*

CHAPTER 23

Bows on a Budget

Student? Just living frugally? Here are some tips
on finding a good, affordable violin bow

BY ERIN SHRADER

broke my first bow on Christmas Eve at the age of 15. It fell on its tip and, to
my horror, the head snapped off. Until that moment I hadn't fully realized
that the bow was not an accessory but a sort of co-instrument with the violin.
Two days later, anxious to begin playing again, I took my great-grandfather's
fiddle to Seattle and made my very first visit to a violin shop. I remember the
light filtering through the dusty leaded glass windows, the aging oriental rugs,
the racks of cellos, a rack of antlers, an old lute, and other instruments I didn't
recognize. It was an utterly arcane world, and standing at the glass counter with
my entire life savings—$62—I realized I had no idea how to go about buying a
bow.

Aspiring string players—or their parents—are routinely confronted with the
necessity of buying a bow on a budget without enough knowledge to make an
informed purchase. A bow can cost anywhere from $50 to tens of thousands and
not look all that different to the untrained eye. What's the difference between a $50
bow and a $150 bow? What can you expect in your price range? What advantages

would just a little bit more money buy? What should you look for in a bow? And for that matter, where do you buy a bow?

CH-CH-CH-CHANGES

The last few years have seen big changes in a traditionally slow-moving trade. Carbon fiber has gained acceptability as an alternative to wood and has recently started coming down in price. The Internet has made good information on bows more accessible and changed the way we shop, while China has emerged as a violin- and bow-making powerhouse. "China has really arrived in the last two or three years," says Jay Ifshin of Ifshin Violins in Berkeley, California, noting that quality has increased dramatically. Like a growing number of retailers, Ifshin runs his own workshop in China, training workers and overseeing production of his own models. "Some teachers get hung up on European," he adds, "but these days Chinese bows are better."

"It's a good situation right now for players," says Todd French, president of StringWorks, a company that designs its own line of instruments and bows. A confluence of conditions currently is working in favor of the consumer, he says, including a low-cost workforce in China and an unfavorable exchange rate with Europe. Quality has increased dramatically, with most work being done by hand rather than machine, while prices have come down. "Who knows how long it will last," says French, whose designs are made by a workshop in China.

The entry-level bow market can be confusing. Entry-level bows are made of several different materials. Prices vary widely and products are frequently not branded but simply labeled with the name of the retailer—if they are stamped at all. To get oriented, we'll start with an explanation of materials, a major factor in price and playability, then describe what to expect in different price ranges.

HOW TO LOOK
෴ AT A BOW ෴

Sight down the bow to see that it is reasonably straight. Tighten the hair. Does the screw turn smoothly? Does the frog move along the stick without twisting from side to side? Does the hair reach playing tension? Is the stick still reasonably straight under tension? If so, you at least have a bow that works.

MATERIALS

While fine bows have been made of one wood, called pernambuco, for the last 200 years, bows for the beginner come in a variety of materials. Pernambuco is prized for its beauty, resilience, and ability to draw tone out of an instrument, but it is also expensive and increasingly endangered. A number of less-

precious materials are suitable for beginners, who may
not be ready to handle the liveliness of pernambuco.

A confluence of conditions is currently working in favor of the consumer.

Leon and Ray Glasser invented the fiberglass bow in
1962, ushering in the use of synthetic materials for bow
making. Fiberglass is a composite of lightweight plastic
reinforced with fine fibers of glass that can then be
molded. The resulting bows have a brighter, less complex
sound than wood, but have the advantage of being
consistent, inexpensive, and virtually indestructible.

 Brazilwood is a generic term for hardwoods from Brazil. Pernambuco is a
single genus of brazilwood, and it grows only in one place: the endangered Mata
Atlantica rainforest on the coast of Brazil. Other brazilwoods grow more widely
and make successful student bows. Excellent-quality brazilwood can be as good or
better than low-grade pernambuco, according to Richard Ward of Ifshin Violins.

Carbon fiber is a later addition to bow making. Carbon fibers are extremely
strong when pulled, but relatively flexible. These fibers can be set in a matrix of
resin by various processes to create a composite material that is both strong and
flexible. The mix of materials can be controlled to achieve specific results. Carbon-
fiber bows vary greatly in price and sophistication, and are typically more
expensive than fiberglass or brazilwood, but have recently entered the beginner
price range.

The frog, where the hair attaches to the bow, is traditionally made of ebony.
Very inexpensive bows sometimes have plastic frogs, while others are made of less
expensive hardwoods. Quality of workmanship varies a great deal. Student bows
are usually "nickel mounted," meaning that the metal parts are made of "nickel
silver," an alloy of nickel, copper, and zinc. Frogs are described as "fully lined" if
they have metal pieces behind the pearl slide and down the back of the frog.
Inexpensive "half-lined" frogs do not have metal behind the slide, resulting in a
lighter- weight frog, which could leave the bow feeling tip-heavy.

Bows with poorly made frogs are time consuming or impossible to rehair.
Workshops are very busy, so cheap bows are often turned away. (A replacement
can often be purchased for $50 or so, about the price of a rehair.) Choose a decent-
quality frog unless you plan to consider the bow disposable. Also, some violin
shops do not work on instruments or bows they did not sell, so they may refer you
to the company that sold it to you—something to consider when shopping. Like
the Sears Roebuck catalog of old, online retailers tend to be less expensive and are
certainly a blessing to those who live in remote areas. In contrast, brick-and-

⌒ BOWS R US ⌒

Pricing of student bows varies greatly. Prices at the low end are highly influenced by market forces such as the cost of labor, currency exchange rates, and the purchasing power of the individual retailer. For simplicity, let's divide the market into four price levels roughly corresponding to $50 increments in price.

Entry Level: About $50

Bows under $50 are typically fiberglass or Chinese-made brazilwood and should at least meet the minimum standards. Fiberglass is virtually

> **At best you may find a good quality brazilwood stick with a fully lined ebony frog.**

indestructible, making it a prudent choice for players too young to resist sword fighting. Wood has a warmer, more interesting sound, but in this price range a certain percentage of bows break under normal playing pressure, says dealer David Kerr of Portland, Oregon, resulting in potential trips to the violin shop for a replacement. "It's up to the person," he says of the choice between wood and fiberglass. Like any reputable shop, Kerr's will replace bows that break under normal use—be sure to ask about that guarantee when you shop.

There are real bargains to be had at this price. At best you may find a good quality brazilwood stick with a fully lined ebony frog. But there are bad bows, too, warns Kerr. At worst, your bargain bow may be unplayable.

Better Beginner: About $100

Expect a better-quality stick that is both stronger and more flexible, better balance from end to frog, and a more complex tone. Also look for better-quality fittings: fully lined ebony frog, metal winding, leather grip.

Sticks in this range are typically better-grade brazilwood, made in China or Germany, or, increasingly, even entry-level pernambuco made in China. Carbon fiber has started to appear in this price range as well. Carbon fiber has the advantage of being almost indestructible, and also impervious to humidity, making it a popular choice as a second bow for advanced players.

Also look for better attention to detail. A nicely carved head is often an indicator of quality work throughout, according to French. The supplier he works with also makes "really, really fine" workshop bows and he finds that their skill trickles down into the lower-end products.

Step-up: About $150

Expect better quality wood with fewer knots and straighter grain, says Val Jaskiewicz, general manager of Shar Products, a long-time mail-order retailer. "Inconsistent wood must be compensated for by hand motion," he continues. High-quality German-made brazilwood and better-grade pernambuco sticks made in China are typical.

Just a Little Bit More...

If you can spend just a little bit more, say in the $200 neighborhood, look for a "a big jump up," says French. Jaskiewicz concurs. He characterizes these higher-grade Chinese-made pernambuco sticks as more responsive, bouncier, more aggressive, and capable of advanced strokes such as sautillè. In this price range, expect significantly better materials, whether German-made brazilwood, pernambuco, or carbon fiber, and still more skilled workmanship.   —E.S.

mortar violin retailers usually maintain a repair shop and priority in the workshop is an unspoken part of the retail price of goods.

SHOPPING!

Bows interact differently with different instruments, so bring your own violin to find the best match. Even among the least expensive wooden bows there is a great deal of variety. Some will be better than others. Ward suggests playing as many bows as possible. "Don't get too hung up on a particular price range," he advises. "Try lots of bows. Come in, try a dozen, take them home for a week, trade them in."

There is no substitute for trying out bows and instruments with the help of a knowledgeable dealer, teacher, or more experienced friend. Every bow is a little different. Learning to see, feel, and hear increasingly subtle differences in quality is also an important part of the progressing player's education.

MINIMUM ∽ STANDARDS ∾

Val Jaskiewicz of Shar Products suggests the following minimum standards for any bow.

The stick should be straight.

It should be strong enough to stand up to normal playing without "giving in" or breaking.

The screw should turn easily. The hair should be real horsehair and not too long. There are synthetics but they don't work as well. If the band of hair is flapping it will not tighten to playing tension.

A version of this chapter originally appeared in the November 2005 issue of Strings *magazine.*

CHAPTER 24

Past Perfect

So you want to get a Baroque bow? Here are a few tips

BY SARAH FREIBERG

I f you enjoy performing music from the Baroque era, but find your modern bow unwieldy in its sometimes complicated passage work, you may be ready to purchase a Baroque bow. If you do, you'll find it easier to maneuver in the intricate slur markings of Bach and his contemporaries. What do you look for in a bow so different from your modern one, and how do you go about selecting your first Baroque bow?

Before Francois Tourte invented the now standard "modern bow" in the late 18th century, there were several styles of bows in circulation. Throughout the Baroque era (approximately 1600–1750), there was little standardization in bows, but most had the distinctive shape and sound of what we now term "Baroque bows." Instead of the familiar concave curve of the modern bow, the Baroque stick curved the other way. Mirroring the curve of the bridge, the early bow was shaped more like an archer's bow, complete with a pointed tip. The earliest Baroque bows tended to be short and sported clip-in frogs. As time went on, bows lengthened. The screw mechanism, allowing for tightening and loosening of the bow hair, appeared around 1700. Baroque bows had less hair than their modern counterparts, and were weighted quite differently, making a natural decrescendo when drawn from frog to tip.

SHOP AROUND

While there are few bows in original Baroque condition available today, there are several bow makers who specialize in making copies of Baroque bows. Ideally, you want to try out a number of different Baroque bows to get a feel for them and find one that is suited to both you and your instrument. If you can attend an early music festival exhibition, you can try bows from many makers at the same time. (Each June, either the Boston or Berkeley Early Music Festival and Exhibition takes place.) If that's not a possibility, try to visit a Baroque bow maker's shop. If you can't go to them, many bow makers will send you bows to try out and compare at home.

A Baroque bow will feel quite different in your hand. Neither the frog nor the tip is as substantial as on a modern bow. Because of the way it is weighted, you may well want to "choke up" on the bow, and bring your hand further up the stick (in the direction of the tip), leaving the frog behind. You want to look for the same things in a Baroque bow as you would in a modern one: It should be responsive, easy to control, and make your instrument sound good. Remember, though, that a Baroque bow does not have the sustaining power of a modern bow. It has less hair, and won't produce a big sound. It will, however, make all those minute slurring details of Baroque music come to life. When trying out possible Baroque bows, be sure to have some suitable period music, such as Bach or Corelli sonatas.

A Baroque bow should produce a nice, consistent sound when drawn from frog to tip—even as it decrescendos. Some bows can be a little *too* responsive, and wobble or skitter at a certain point, often towards the tip end. Unless you feel you can control that skittery area, you might want to try a different bow.

If possible, search out the advice of someone who specializes in Baroque music. Find out what kind of bow he or she prefers—maybe have him or her try the bows for you. I know that when I bought my first Baroque bow, I didn't really know what to look for—I trusted a friend who sold me *her* first Baroque bow. It was solid, and stood me in good stead for a number of years. I later sold it to one of my students, continuing its chain of becoming another cellist's first Baroque bow.

One of my colleagues said "your first Baroque bow is really a throwaway." Her point was that you really learn how to use a Baroque bow by playing on one. In time, as you become more adept with that bow, you may find you've outgrown it, and want to trade up. It's always a good idea to see if a maker will take a bow back in trade if you purchase another bow from him or her. Remember, a bow is as individual as you are, so don't hurry into a decision. Happy experimenting!

A version of this chapter originally appeared in the May/June 2002 issue of Strings *magazine.*

CHAPTER 25

Elements of Sound

Carbon-fiber bows gain ground with a growing cadre of cellists

BY HEATHER K. SCOTT

N ot that I want or need a carbon-fiber bow any more than I want or need a wooden leg," one classically trained cellist remarked recently about his experience with carbon-fiber bows. This stigma, once prevalent in the world of stringed instruments, is quickly falling by the wayside. With each passing year, more and more violin dealers sell a steadily increasing number of carbon-fiber bows—a testament to many players' need for inexpensive, extremely durable, good-sounding bows.

"My impression is that players are becoming more open to the idea of carbon-fiber bows and what they offer," says Susan Horkan, formerly of Johnson String Instrument in Newton, Massachusetts. "The availability of these bows has never been a problem," adds John C. Jordan, owner of Jordan Violins in Concord, California, "but I notice them gaining acceptance and market share in recent years."

Strings asked a panel of professional players to sample several carbon-fiber bows for intermediate- and advanced-level cellists. Our panel consisted of three professional cellists: Sandy Wilson of the Alexander String Quartet (playing an H.

Silvestre, 1864 cello); Paul Hale of the Philharmonia Baroque Orchestra, American Bach Soloists, California Symphony, and Oakland Symphony (Joseph Grubaugh & Sigrun Seifert, ten-year-old poplar-back cello); and Mark Summer of the Turtle Island Quartet (Joseph Grubaugh & Sigrun Seifert, 1997).

Once thought to be the best material for students' and beginners' bows—it is unflaggingly durable—carbon fiber is emerging as the material of choice for professionals seeking a second bow, as well as a primary bow for many musicians in general. "I find that professional musicians want an alternative bow that has the response and playability of a higher-quality stick and can be used in situations where a more expensive pernambuco wood bow would incur a greater risk of damage, such as outdoor concerts," says Horkan.

While our reviewers were quite taken by a couple of the more expensive models, all agreed that there are real bargains to be found among the more affordable bows.

Our panel evaluated bows for their quality of sound, aesthetics, technical specifications, and price (ranging from approximately $300 to $3,000). The examples presented here do not constitute a complete list—there are dozens of additional companies offering carbon-fiber models for all levels of musicians. While *Strings* made an effort to include all of the leading manufacturers in this survey, several companies did not respond to our participation requests. The following makers were not included in this survey: Berg Bows, Durro Bows, and ARY France. *Strings* also received a couple of bows that we couldn't include in this review. Difficulties adjusting the end button on our sample Leopold bow prevented us from maintaining taut hair. (A problem most likely due to the glue inside the button losing grip of the screw, and easily fixed by any violin maker. Leopold assures us that the life-long warranty covers all repairs. For more information, visit www.leopold-bow.com.) We also received a bow from Carbow LNM, but it arrived with transport damage, and we were unable to acquire a replacement in time for our panelists to review. (See www.carbow.com.)

ARCUS

Bernd Müsing and Andreas Wetzlinger have been producing Arcus bows for five years in their factory workshop in Klagenfurt, Austria. The bows purport to be especially light and agile due to their hollow core. We looked at five of Arcus' latest cello bow designs.

Wilson professionally endorses Arcus bows—and has used them often in the past when making studio recordings. But he admittedly didn't care for the cutaway frog or the new opaque color of the stick (until last March Arcus painted all its sticks a shiny black—but, since then, the company has left them with a polished-carbon finish). He adds, "There is no leverage for my little finger."

Hale enjoyed the light Arcus models, but also questions the cutaway design of the frog on the newer models, saying, "This just doesn't seem comfortable."

The Concerto bow was a favorite from the Arcus collection, for its smooth sound and playability.

Concerto, $1,995. *Ten-year warranty (stick). 65–70 grams. Carbon-fiber, octagonal stick; sterling silver wrap; leather grip; snakewood frog; mother-of-pearl eye; titanium underslide; snakewood and silver button. (We also looked at the Cadenza Gold $3,540, Cadenza Silver $2,900, Sinfonia $1,455, and Sonata $970.) Distributed by J. Fenn Inc. (800) 883-3606; or Arcus, 49 (931) 95 00 602, www.arcus-bow.de.*

CODABOW

The panel tried several CodaBow models, but gravitated to two in particular: the Electric and the Classic. The Electric is the newest addition to the CodaBow line, and is specially designed to be played with electric cello (although we tried it with acoustic instruments). CodaBow began business in 1993 with the mission of creating "a family of bows for stringed instruments that would serve the performance needs of all serious players and rival the finest existing pernambuco bows available."

"Feels good," says Hale of the flashy purple Electric model. "I like the color."

Wilson agrees, saying, "This purple thing has guts."

"Clean, but slow," says Hale of the Classic, his preferred choice of the CodaBows. "Just a tad slower. But that can be nice, too. It is more lush sounding."

Summer, a long-time user and endorser of CodaBows, also likes the Classic. "This draws a bassier, deeper sound," he observes. "And it definitely is a nice looking stick."

Wilson isn't as sure of the Classic's balance or sound. "I'm just not confident going to the tip," he comments. But he adds, "There's nothing wrong with it, really; sometimes the chemistry is just not right."

Jordan Violins reports that CodaBows achieve healthy sales at its retail shop. "The [CodaBow models] that I've sold have gone mostly to serious amateurs and semi-professional players in both classical and popular music styles," says Jordan. "Some were used as primary bows and others as specific-purpose bows, such as for playing in an orchestra pit for a theater where space is confined and a wooden bow is more at risk of damage."

Electric, $365. Limited warranty (shaft only); 79.5 grams; purple dyno-chromatic, round, carbon-fiber stick; silver-thread wrap; leather-foam grip; engineered ebony frog with nickel-silver fittings; "electrified" CodaBow signature inlay; pearl slide; nickel-silver button.

Classic, $925. Full lifetime guarantee to registered owner and priority workshop service privilege, 80.5 grams; polished graphite (ebony) finish, round, carbon-fiber stick; sterling silver wrap; Moroccan goat skin grip; ebony frog; gold "Coda" eye inlay; abalone heart slide; three-part sterling silver and ebony button with abalone eye. (We also looked at the Aspire, $325, and the Conservatory, $520.) Available from CodaBow, (888) 263-2269, www.codabow.com.

EASTMAN

Eastman Strings is a new producer of carbon-fiber bows, having just released its Cadenza line in 2003. We took a look at all four models: the Prelude, Artist, Silver, and Master. Our reviewers were impressed with the samples we received, finding them to be a good value for all players.

"This is a very nice bow, actually," says Summer of the Silver. "It is bouncy, and a little hard to control—but not overly so. I like this bow, not a bad stick at all."

Wilson comments on the bows' design—noting the well-constructed, close seat of the frog to the stick (some bows display a gap or looseness here, a common problem with some carbon-fiber bows). And each one produced a smooth, warm sound on both Hale's and Wilson's instruments.

"This is shaky in the middle," Hale reports. "But I'd rather have that than something totally dead. It is very slight and I could get used to it."

"Wow, for these prices, I think they are incredible," says Hale of the Eastman line. "So many cheap wood bows don't have any mass to them, but at least with a carbon-fiber bow you have the density without the stiffness. These are flexible and even from frog to tip."

"They all feel pretty similar," Wilson responds after picking up several of the Eastman bows. "For the money, I think these are fine."

Cadenza Silver, $475. Lifetime warranty for stick; approx. 82 grams; black, round, carbon-fiber stick; silver wire wrap; leather grip; ebony frog with silver ferrule and heel plate; Parisian-style abalone eye; silver ring; abalone slide; silver button with abalone eye. (We also looked at the Cadenza Prelude, $205, Cadenza Artist, $325, and the Cadenza Master, $750). Available from Eastman Strings, (800) 624-0270, www.eastmanstrings.com.

J.S. FINKEL HYBRID

These unique hybrids—combining a carbon-fiber core with an exterior shell of pernambuco—are billed on the Finkel website as suitable "for an advancing student's first pernambuco wood bow or an established player's reliable second practice bow." Johannes S. Finkel invented this bow in his traditional workshop in Switzerland. Finkel also states on his website that the hybrid design will prevent the stick from warping and aid in consistent playability.

"I like the stick," says Hale of the Finkel's unique design. "I love the feel of it so far. I imagine after the hair is broken in it will feel better. It isn't too heavy. Lively. Feels like it has potential."

Summer likes the feel of the bow, calling it a "powerful stick. This has a noticeably warm tone," he adds.

Wilson is equally intrigued by the hybrid quality of this bow and wonders about its construction—a company trade secret.

∽ HOW CARBON-FIBER BOWS ARE MADE ∽

The production of carbon-fiber bows involves a peculiar mix of craftsmanship and rocket science. When people talk about nonwood bows, they usually refer to those made of a wide range of synthetic materials, including fiberglass and carbon fiber, a polymer which is a form of graphite.

The type of fiber used in the carbon-fiber bows discussed in this article is called a "pan" fiber, one that is thermally stable and resists change chemically. Carbon fiber, or composite material as it is sometimes called, is made up of two major components: a reinforcing fiber and a matrix, or resin. When mixed together, these ingredients produce a material with mechanical properties that far exceed their individual strengths.

The manufacturing process begins with a thread of carbon-based material that is run through a sophisticated oven. There the nascent fiber is stretched and heated—a process that's called pyrolysis—in an oxygen-free, nitrogen-rich environment. As the fiber stretches, extraneous atoms burn off until a new carbon-based substance forms.

Manufacturers must then decide what to add to the recipe to produce a composite material that suits their specific bow design. Resins are an important part of this stage, since they act as the glue that holds the carbon fibers together.

The carbon mixture is poured into a mold and heated until the ingredients solidify. The resins surrounding the carbon fibers are "thermal set"— they cure when heated and can't revert to their previous state. This produces a highly durable, yet very flexible, composite material.

To produce a good composite structure for bow making, the manufacturers accentuate the stiffness-to-weight ratio—while reaching for the desired acoustic characteristics. Some bow-making companies strive for strict standards with every bow they produce, while others choose to make a less expensive product and accept a certain level of inconsistency.

J.S. Finkel, $2,195. Approx. 81 grams. Round, pernambuco and carbon-fiber hybrid stick; silver wrap and tip; leather grip; ebony frog; Parisian-style pearl eye; silver-mounted pearl slide; silver button. Available from Finkel Bows, (41) 33 951 15 09, www.finkel-bows.ch.

CLAUDIO RIGHETTI ARC VERONA (SARTORY)

Claudio Righetti patented his first usable carbon-fiber bow in 1989, and his synthetic bows have been in production ever since. We received three models for evaluation—the Sartory, Lamy, and D.Peccatte. "These are all superior bows," says Wilson of the collection. "I'm going to come back [to each] and play them again."

Of all the Righetti bows we tested, the Sartory—the newest of the bunch—was by far the most popular. "This is nice! A light bow. For me, it is more lively and responsive. It feels like at any moment you can do something with the bow," Hale explains. "It feels quick and fun, very flexible but strong. There is no shake in the middle for me, like with the others."

"I like how this bow bounces," reports Summer.

The Righetti bows in general proved to be favorites for both Wilson and Hale (who returned to our offices several days later to play them once again). The trio of sticks all produced warm sounds with clear tone. Easy manageability was noted by each reviewer (aside from the small wiggle in the middle of the Lamy bow, noticed by Hale), and a nice balance from frog to tip. Aesthetically, they agree, these bows are very attractive—the design is clean and traditional.

Sartory, $2,300. Lifetime warranty against breakage, 78–84 grams, round, carbon-fiber, reddish-brown stick, silver wrap; lizard skin grip; silver-mounted ebony frog; Parisian-style mother-of-pearl eye and slide; silver button. (We also looked at the Lamy, $1,900, and the D. Pecatte, $2,150.) Available in the US from Johnson String Instrument, or from Arc Verona, (39) 045 8004614 , www.arcverona.com.

SPICCATO FRENCH-AMERICAN BOWS

Spiccato bows were designed and created by master French archetier Benoît Rolland, and are produced and distributed by Spiccato Bows in Salt Lake City. We took a look at the Premiere Silver, Arpège Silver, and Arpège Nickel Silver models. The Premiere employs a camber-adjustment system. By turning the key clockwise, the adjuster "tightens and bends the bow, increasing sensitivity and agility," according to the company literature. When the key is turned counterclockwise, "the bow becomes more stable."

"The Spiccato bows are a recent addition to [our] inventory and thus far the feedback . . . has been extremely favorable," says Horkan of the Spiccato bows we reviewed. "Players find these sticks to be very strong and responsive, and pull a clear, full tone from the instruments. A wide range of players have purchased these bows from beginners to professionals," she adds.

Wilson concurs: "My sense is that [Spiccato] bows are made in a more exacting sort of way."

But Hale isn't as impressed with the Spiccato bows. "This is heavier at the tip," he says of the Premiere. "All of [the Spiccato bows] are not necessarily to my liking. But they are very lively—more so than I would have guessed."

Siding with Hale, Summer likes the sound of the Spiccato, but isn't fond of the weight. "This is fine and good," he notes, "but I wonder why it is so heavy."

Wilson enjoys being able to adjust the camber of the Premiere, and he's drawn to the workmanship of the three bows we tested. "Not an inch of bow is wasted here," he says. "They seem to be made with a fine tolerance."

Premiere silver (adjustable camber), $1,748. *Limited lifetime warranty; 78–84 grams; round, carbon-fiber, reddish-brown stick (Peccate/Maline–style head); silver wrap and tip; leather grip; silver-mounted ebony frog; Parisian-style goldfish eye, silver and pearl button. (We also looked at the Arpège nickel silver, $652, and the Arpège silver, $998). Available from Spiccato French-American Bows, (801) 537-7856, www.prierviolins.com, www.spiccato.com.*

YAMAHA

Another company new to carbon-fiber production, Yamaha released two models in 2003. According to the company, Yamaha began manufacturing carbon-fiber bows to "protect the diminishing supplies of pernambuco wood." These new bows are priced very reasonably. The main difference between the two we looked at is in the aesthetics—the more expensive CBB-305 model has silver fittings, instead of nickel. It is important to note the price of these bows—they are some of the lowest we reviewed, on a par with the Eastman models.

"This bounces nicely," states Summer. "It's a bright-sounding bow."

"Both of the [Yamaha] models are lightweight, but not quite balanced right," says Wilson.

"This feels good; I think it's a nice bow," Hale says of the CBB-305. "It doesn't have any weird shakes to it. It's more controlled when compared to some of these other bows. It seems like a nice stick. It also has a focused intent from the frog to tip—like any good bow."

CBB-305, $2,195. *Ten-year warranty, approx. 78–84 grams. Round, carbon-fiber stick; silver wrap; leather grip; ebony frog; abalone eye with silver ring; abalone slide with silver accent; silver button with abalone inlay and ebony core. (We also looked at the CBB-301, $495). Available from Yamaha Music Corporation, (714) 522-9011, www.yamaha.com.*

A version of this chapter originally appeared in the April 2004 issue of Strings *magazine. Since this chapter ran, advances in carbon-fiber technology (such as braiding and the use of pernambuco veneers) have widened the range of options available. Visit the* Strings *archives at www.stringsmagazine.com to learn more about new products and advances in this technology.*

Section 4

Buying
Accessories

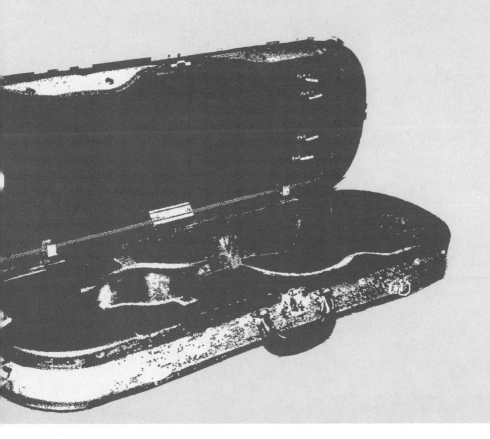

CHAPTER 26

Case-by-Case Basis

Pointers on selecting a new instrument case

BY ERIN SHRADER

I magine trying to carry your violin and bows to rehearsal without a case. Clearly, a case is indispensable, but selecting a new one presents a formidable challenge. The array of materials, shapes, and features available is bewildering. Cases range from simple to sumptuous, with prices starting at $24.95 and climbing into the thousands—and nearly all provide adequate protection. Choosing wisely requires balancing several factors: strength, weight, features, durability, and price. Understanding how a case works, how you will use it, plus identifying personal preferences will help you narrow the field.

MODERN CASE CONSTRUCTION

In terms of protection, today's cases are a vast improvement over anything available a few decades ago. Most come with sturdy, water-resistant nylon canvas covers. This is your first line of defense against dirt and weather. The zippers help hold the case shut and D-rings for straps attach to this cover.

The shell protects against impact. The strongest are made of laminated wood, but technology has produced lightweight synthetic and composite materials of excellent strength, including various types of foam, wood-and-foam laminates, Kevlar, and Teflon. A highly arched top adds strength as well as allowing more room between the top of the case and the bridge area. The lightest cases are constructed of foam and weigh as little as 3.5 pounds. The hardest cases weigh over twice as much.

Virtually all modern cases, regardless of price, employ a suspension system. The violin is held in place by a neck strap and "suspended" on a system of foam pads that prevent it from touching the hard shell of the case. Suspension greatly reduces damage because the shock of impact is not transmitted to the instrument.

There is no reason not to buy a suspension case.

FEATURES

Beyond protection, cases offer many special features. Consider where you live, how you travel, personal style, and what you carry in the way of bows and accessories. Is extreme weather an issue? Look for rain flaps, extra insulation, or perhaps a hygrometer and humidifier for combating dryness. Will you commute with your case, or tour? Choose for maximum durability and safety. How do you travel? If you walk everywhere, the case must be comfortable to carry. Do you keep music and electronic equipment in your case, or are you hoping to reduce the clutter? Shaped cases are lighter and less expensive; oblongs accommodate more bows, plus your portfolio. Crescent shapes are an attractive compromise. Style and materials can reflect personality, from high-tech to traditional, outrageous to refined.

A CASE TO LAST, OR A CASE TO LAST 'A WHILE'?

An inexpensive case will protect your violin, but will wear out fairly quickly. One option is to buy inexpensive cases and replace them as needed. Quality components and workmanship cost more but will last for many years. Zippers break even on the finest cases, so find out if the company makes replacement covers.

THE RIGHT CASE FOR YOU

Violist Wanda Law of the San Diego Symphony suggests "shopping backstage" among your friends. You can examine details, make sure everything fits, and get first-person consumer reports. Law finds her ultralight foam case, made by Toshira (3.5 pounds, $89.95 from the Shar Products Co.), quite adequate against everyday bumps and scrapes. Her informal survey of the orchestra reveals many ultralight cases.

"They're especially popular with older players," she says, "who often have shoulder problems."

On the other hand, "There's no protection in those!" declares LeRoy Weber, inventor of the suspension case. Weber regularly receives letters from grateful patrons whose violins survive terrible accidents in his outstanding cases.

Only you can determine the combination of safety, price, and convenience that will keep you and your violin comfortable. Luckily, if you know what you want, chances are good that it's available.

A version of this chapter originally appeared in the June/July 2005 issue of Strings *magazine.*

CHAPTER 27

Lap of Luxury

Black German velvet? Custom inlay or gold fittings?
Tough enough to survive a car crash? Buying an instrument case—
when money is no object

BY ERIN SHRADER

Case shopping is usually an exercise in compromise, balancing weight
against protection, carrying capacity, comfort, and price. We take a deep
breath and choose between the black cover and the grey, sigh, and resign
ourselves to repeating the whole exercise in a few years when the new case wears
out, wishing secretly for just a little bit of . . . style.

What if you could have it all?

Safe enough for a Strad, lightweight, elegant, in the material of your choice—
with even a special place for your eyeglasses? What if you saw your beloved
instrument luxuriously ensconced in your favorite colors, every day? In a case built
to last a lifetime?

What if price were no object?

Chances are your dream could be made real by one of a small, international
cadre of craftsmen who build cases worthy of the rarest violins. Several of them
are, in fact, violin makers who found themselves intrigued with the unexplored
creative potential in cases: the satisfaction of solving a design problem, improved

safety for the violins they love, an outlet for the artistic eye, and an untapped market. The best case makers combine the skills of an engineer, entrepreneur, woodworker, inventor, and interior designer.

Small wonder that violin making alone did not contain their curiosity and creativity.

The difference is not always obvious at first glance (indeed, commercial manufacturers are constantly taking their cues from these innovators). But closer inspection reveals a level of ingenuity, attention to detail, and elegance that makes ordinary cases seem, well, ordinary.

Compared to the price of a major repair, fine cases are a bargain. Some case makers mentioned in this article offer simple but elegant and extremely safe models starting at around $600. And $900 to $1,200 should buy a very stylish off-the-shelf model, while made-to-fit and custom models cost more. How much more? That depends on your taste.

Skilled craftsmanship and fine materials make an immediate impression. Cordura—the same rugged synthetic material used in US Army backpacks—is the nearly unanimous exterior fabric of choice, although Negri makes a case in leather. Covers fit perfectly with seams neatly trimmed in materials that will not crack with age. D-rings for carrying straps will never come off. Interior compartments close smoothly with just the right amount of resistance.

Flawlessly executed upholstery work makes even the simplest interiors a delight to behold. Individualism and tradition reach a harmonious balance in the choice of interior materials. Among the options are sumptuous silk velvet, natural cotton suede and velour, glove leather, and all manners of satin. Maurizio and Carla Riboni's cases are lined in solid colors accompanied by a patterned silk blanket. Case maker Dimitri Musafia had satin woven with the design inlaid on the 1677 "Sunrise" Strad. LeRoy Weber is experimenting with nature scenes inside the top, just for fun, and the truly adventurous can check out the "exotics" page on his website (www.weberscases.com) for inspiration.

Some makers will give a customer free rein with interior materials while others insist on maintaining at least veto power over potential fashion disasters. It takes experience to know what will and will not make a beautiful violin case. "In the end, it's my name that goes onto the case!" says Musafia, who learned that lesson the hard way when a famous fashion designer who commissioned a case insisted on heavy, stiff materials that were virtually unworkable. Still, interior design and amenities are arenas where the case maker's ingenuity can shine and wishes can be granted.

For musicians who "live" in their cases, thoughtful details can make life on the road just a little easier.

When Isaac Stern came to Weber for one of the very first suspension cases, he requested a mirror, a place for his comb, and a holder for his eyeglasses. Weber not only invented the suspension case, he also put hygrometers and humidifiers in his models, and added subway handles. A look at the 600 series confirms that he has considered every possible way a case might be carried. His most recent invention is a holder for the shoulder rest that folds neatly under the neck of the instrument, freeing up compartment space.

Musafia offers an accessory compartment that will light up upon opening so you can find your necessities backstage, while Alexander Caballero will fit a reflective strip unobtrusively into the binding of his case covers for musicians in Switzerland who commute by bicycle.

Quality fittings are another signature of cases built to last. For example, the cool, slate-colored latch of a Michael Gordge case clicks smoothly shut like the lock on a bank vault. Musicians love Riboni's distinctive leather-wound chrome handles and padded straps, according to instrument dealer Claire Givens, who offers their cases in her Minneapolis violin shop. Musafia handles are screwed on rather than riveted, which eliminates the need to damage the case simply to replace the hardware.

Caballero takes this one step further and sinks receptors into the wood so there will be no future damage from new screws. He also uses three hinges instead of two. Ribbon stops take the strain off the hinges, increasing longevity.

Gordge cases come with leather carrying straps, and use leather for compartment handles, zipper pulls, and ties to hold the neck in place.

Brass corner guards protect the corners of Riboni's bow cases.

"There is a responsibility in manufacturing to protect the instrument for the time it rests within the case," says Dominik Musafia. His brother's cases have been entrusted with the protection of many of the world's great instruments. One of those is "The Cannon," Paganini's legendary del Gesù. "The case we made for the Cannon was custom-made to measure, with reinforcements against impact, thermal insulation (which we call 'Tropicalization'), and all the safety features we normally put into a high-end case," says Dimitri Musafia. "Basically, it was a case that anyone can buy, except that we used a specially milled silk velvet with a pattern that I designed and had produced."

Elegant finishes and thoughtful amenities may delight the user, but the case maker's best efforts go unnoticed until disaster strikes. "'If I treat it well nothing will happen,' that's what people think," stresses Weber. "But accidents happen." He illustrates that point with the example of a young violist whose father fell asleep at the wheel. "It was a terrible accident, the car was totaled," he relates. The viola was thrown out of the car and landed some distance away, the case punctured. "The kid was still in the hospital when the father brought me the case. He was afraid to open it." The viola had been merely knocked out of tune.

He made the family a new case.

In the never-ending tug of war between weight and protection, cases have undergone great structural design changes in recent years. After many experiments, wood remains the preferred shell material, with several makers using lightweight six-ply poplar laminates. Reevaluating the distribution of that wood—adding layers in the most vulnerable areas while lightening the areas that take less impact—has resulted in greater protection with less weight.

Weber raised the arch in the top of his 600 series, further increasing strength. Since joints are the weakest point, corners, which take the most impact, are bent rather than joined like a picture frame. Where joining is necessary, Caballero uses

⤳ WHATEVER-PROOF ↶

Dimitri Musafia was having trouble with his new elliptical-shaped violin cases—he kept dropping them. He'd been toying with the idea of an elliptical case with the violin offset inside (smaller, lighter, more room for accessories) for about 14 years. But he kept dropping them, and they kept breaking. True, they were being dropped out of a Porsche going 100 mph, but still . . . Musafia reasoned, they shouldn't break.

When a case finally survived the crash test, remaining completely intact, he put it into production.

The same vivid imagination that goes into design goes into Musafia's product testing. To test the durability of a new case-cover material, he nailed a violin case to the roof of a house in Long Beach, California, where it was exposed to salt air, the occasional severe rainstorm, and summertime rooftop temperatures routinely climbing to around 120 degrees Fahrenheit. Waterproof cases were floated in the harbor, just to make sure they really were waterproof. Cases were lined up in the hot sun with thermometers to measure the benefits of "tropicalization," a foam and ultrathin aluminum film insulation available as a custom option on most models.

However extreme these measures may sound, they make sense. A high-quality case isn't merely a luxurious indulgence; it's an investment in the safety of your instrument. You're not only buying a thing of beauty, but also the highest quality materials and, most of all, expertise—the case maker's years of experience, skill, and understanding.

You might want to think twice about tossing a fine violin out of a speeding Porsche, but it's reassuring to know that in the right case, it might just make it.   —E.S.

special waterproof glue, and he clamps rather than stapling the pieces together for gluing. You can work more quickly with staples, he says, but staples corrode over time, weakening the structure.

The shapes and layouts of cases are evolving, as well. The Ribonis further rounded off the corners, making a more oblong shape that is structurally sound and also lighter and more compact than the traditional rectangular shape. Tilting the instrument inside the case allowed a gracefully curved interior compartment in the newest Musafia model. Musafia managed to fit a smallish viola into a violin-size shell to reduce weight for an injured violist. Riboni's small, lightweight double-violin case is the size of a viola, making it easier to bring onto airplanes, according to violin maker Joan Balter, of Berkeley, California. "Speaking as a dealer, this makes such a nice presentation," she adds, appreciating the tastefully understated style.

Weber relocated the large accessory compartment, traditionally found above the scroll, to the opposite end of the case. Should a bow spinner let go, the frog would fall harmlessly on the compartment lid rather than damaging the violin.

Aside from structural improvements and the suspension pads that are now virtually universal, additional safety features can be built into cases. Musafia offers several as custom options on any of its cases, including waterproofing, special puncture-resistant fabric, a valance-and-groove closure, and "tropicalization," an additional layer of padding and space-blanket–like material under the cover that slows down changes in temperature. Riboni cases can be ordered with a combination-lock or alarm system.

Some companies simply offer excellent quality in their standard models. Others welcome custom work. "I like seeing the people happy," admits Caballero, whose clientele includes dealers, soloists, and orchestra players. The best way to get a Caballero case is to visit his atelier in Lucerne, Switzerland, near the concert hall. Like an appointment with the dressmaker, a picture is drawn, the instrument's measurements taken, colors and materials chosen. Then your case is made while you are in town.

Although he is a successful bow maker and Cremonese-trained violin maker, "I enjoy my time making cases like bows," he says. "I make cases out of passion."

Sometimes the greatest reward for that effort is the smile of the recipient. Caballero once built a case commissioned for presentation as a gift to a well-known musician who was quite indifferent to the idea. "We knew the favorite colors of this person. We made this case with mahogany, hand polished with shellac. Black German velvet . . . and gold pins with imitations of diamonds on the tops."

Seeing the inside of the case, the player exclaimed, "This is the most beautiful case I have ever seen!" The violinist immediately put the Strad in the case and offered a beautiful smile.

Musafia offers several standard lines, but all can be ordered with custom options. He enjoys a challenge, such as weighing every component of a case to engineer the absolute lightest case for that injured violist. Or the three-year collaboration with virtuoso violinist Salvatore Accardo, which completely changed the structural design of Musafia cases. The case maker concludes, "Making violin and viola cases one-at-a-time and allowing for their customization is not the most efficient and profitable way to produce them, but it is certainly the most creative and gratifying. I have dedicated my life to artistically crafting violin and viola cases as best as I can and take great pride in doing so."

LeRoy Weber has also dedicated much of his career to making the best possible case. Nearing retirement age, he recently downsized the case-making operation and returned to his early love, violin restoration. He now makes all the cases himself, and most are custom orders.

"They all end up being a little different, anyway," he says, as he continues to think of improvements to be made.

A version of this chapter originally appeared in the April 2005 issue of Strings *magazine.*

CHAPTER 28

Grab Bag

Gig bags and case covers make life easier
for pros and students alike

BY HEATHER K. SCOTT

F or musicians with hectic schedules, finding a safe and convenient carrying system for a violin, viola, cello, or bass can be difficult. Busy students and professionals jumping from taxi to bus to subway and back again need to have hands free not just for balance and stability on bumpy public-transit rides, but also to juggle cell phones, PDAs, and other travel essentials. A gig bag or case cover can transform a bulky case into a convenient backpack, provide added protection to a travel case, or act as an alternative mode of instrument transportation between gigs.

How do you know if a gig bag is right for you?

Maybe you have a battered old case that you've fallen in love with over the years, despite its being heavy and bulky, and you just can't part with it. Perhaps you're looking for a quick slipcover to protect your cello between late-night gigs. Or possibly your pocketbook just doesn't allow for a new lighter-weight case. Gig bags and case covers are a reasonably priced way to upgrade your current case, or transport your instrument around town without the added bulk of a hard case.

Matt Stamell of Stamell String Instruments in Amherst, Massachusetts, says most of the players who visit his shop looking for gig bags and case covers are professionals and preprofessionals. Their reasons? "To protect their cases and to give extra carrying capability," he says.

"Hard-shell cases, especially with the larger instruments, are quite unmanageable for some," adds Simon McHugh of McHugh Violin Shop in Wichita, Kansas.

Some musicians feel that gig bags and case covers are even a worthy replacement for the traditional case, especially when it comes to hauling unwieldy basses. "Bass padded covers are the most practical and safest means of protective 'everyday' transport of the bass violin," says Barrie Kolstein of Kolstein Music, Inc.

WHAT TO LOOK FOR

"I am looking for quality construction with good protection for my instrument; light weight and easy to carry—also easy and safe to pack and unpack," notes Dorothy Cole, a String Talk forum member (at www.stringsmagazine.com) and cellist with the Charlotte Symphony in North Carolina. Cole is not alone in her quest for a light, safe, and convenient way to transport her instrument. Such requests are the reason most musicians begin their search for a gig bag or case cover.

But what should you look for when evaluating these products?

Stamell says most of his clients are looking for "good-quality construction, good padding, and large pockets for music and accessories."

"Padding is always a prime concern, particularly in cello and bass covers," reports Tom Kagan of T.R. Kagan Violins in Raleigh, North Carolina. "Bow pockets, rather than a detachable bow case/pouch, are favored, as are pockets for rosin, spare strings, and bridges."

Tony Nigliazzo, a violinist and String Talk contributor, sees zippers as the most important aspect of any case cover or gig bag. When a zipper broke on his case last season, the violinist says he suffered a "catastrophic failure" that irreparably damaged his instrument.

For McHugh, the most important traits of a good gig bag or case cover include "serious protection for the instrument, generous accessory/bow pockets, and, above all, substantial zippers." But he adds this caveat: "Give serious thought to the amount of convenience balanced with the exposure to damage. A hard-shell case is hard to beat for best protection."

When shopping for your own gig bag or case cover, take along an evaluation check-list. Case manufacturer Barrie Kolstein recommends "[looking] at the overall structural quality of the cover, the amenities and the features of the cover, and the aesthetics."

You'll also want to consider the padded and/or insulated linings; reinforced seams and linings; extra-strong zippers; multiple, reinforced, and well-positioned handles; comfortable padded shoulder or backpack straps; and bow, accessory, and/or music pockets.

THE PERFECT MATCH

Some musicians find it difficult to nail down that "perfect" bag. Straps may be well-padded and handles well-placed, but the lining may not be as thick as you'd like. Or size may even be an issue, as it was for *Strings* reader Annyta Klein Vizard.

"We recently bought a cello and found it difficult—impossible—to find a bag case that fit," Vizard laments. "The cello is larger than most and we had to go with a larger, heavier, hard case instead of a lighter padded case. We wish that all cases had a place for music and rosin while protecting the instrument."

Natalie Haas, a professional cellist and Juilliard School graduate, finally settled on a case cover. "I use something called the 'Blobby'—we nicknamed it 'Dobby the Blobby'—to fly with over my Alan Stevenson cello case," she shares. "It's a big black denim bag that insulates the case with solid foam on all sides. Dobby and I have a love/hate relationship . . . never once has my cello been harmed when I check it, but it is the most ridiculous thing to carry. It only weighs 35 pounds total with cello, case, and Blobby, but it is huge . . . and it doesn't have wheels! Still, it's worth all the awkwardness to know that my cello is safe."

Haas purchased her Blobby from case maker Alan Stevenson.

James Lyon, a professor of violin at Penn State University, found success with a case cover as well. "I love my Cushy! Its padding keeps my Vuillaume safe from extreme weather and cushions any small impacts incurred in transit. The strap is also totally reliable, unlike the one that came with my case . . . . The Cushy case cover, easily slips over any standard full-size oblong violin case and I definitely recommend it!" The Cushy is available from Shar Music.

Sarah Freiberg, a professional cellist and frequent *Strings* contributor, instead finds gig bags are better suited to her needs. "I have a top-of-the-line well-padded soft cello case by Reunion Blues that I have taken on the road with me," she says. "I just use that instead of a hard case when I'm flying and have a seat for the cello. I remember once flying a red-eye from California to Boston with my infant son, who didn't have a seat, and the cello, which did have a seat. Because of airline regulations at the time, I had been bumped to first class so that the cello could have a proper seat; soon after I got on the plane, an attendant offered to stow the cello in a closet. So, my son ended up with the seat and the cello was safely stowed."

She adds, "Sometimes, if I have to take my cello on a flight, but it doesn't have a seat, I send it underneath in a big case, but pack my Reunion Blues case in luggage so that I can use it at my destination."

BETTER SHOP AROUND

Like shopping for any instrument accessory, it will take time to locate the best gig bag or case cover for your purposes. If you find yourself looking at a variety of brands and wishing you could take the zipper off one, the handles from another, and the lining from still another, you'll be glad to learn that there are companies that will take your favorite qualities and design a custom gig bag or case cover.

One such firm is the Mooradian Cover Company. In business for more than 25 years, Mooradian was the first company to use mountain-climbing materials in its production of gig bags. Today the innovative company offers custom services in addition to its standard product line. You can discuss the qualities you want in a bag or cover, submit your instrument measurements, and Mooradian will create a bag based on your specifications. (The company also makes bags for gambas, basses, and viols.)

If having a custom case made doesn't fit your pocketbook, consider what String Talk member Kevin Thomson did to solve his own "Frankenstein" dilemma.

After growing concerned over not being able to find a case cover or gig bag that wasn't black, which, Thomson says, "as you well know [is] subject to substantial heat gain, even when carried in an air conditioned car, I was a little leary of transporting my wife's $3,000 [instrument] in her black case on a family vacation."

Rather than give up the fight, Thomson devised his own custom case cover.

"I went to my local Ace Hardware," he says, "and bought some Reflectex brand silver-coated, bubble-wrap insulation. I also purchased a stick-on zipper [to use as a cover closure] that was designed to stick to plastic sheeting for construction-site door covers; you just stick the zipper over your plastic dust barrier, unzip it, and then cut a 'doorway' with a sharp knife. I took the Reflectex and cut a shape to the form of my case, taped it all together with the metal-foil tape I had also purchased, stuck the zipper on the side, cut it open and voilá! I had an insulated, reflecting, affordable case cover that protected my wife's [instrument] and case to a T!"

Like the old adage says, where there's a will, there's a way.

A version of this chapter originally appeared in the January 2005 issue of Strings *magazine.*

CHAPTER 29

Rest Assured

Choosing the chin rest that best suits your needs

BY MARY NEMET

Paganini, the greatest violinist of all time, never once used a chin rest. The great maestro—known for his blistering speed and devilishly aggressive attack—was able to push his left shoulder so far forward that the violin rested on his collarbone. But, despite this exception, most violinists and violists now accept the chin rest as a useful ally in correctly and comfortably positioning the instrument.

But who first thought of this handy invention? And how did it come to be such an integral part of violinists' and violists' lives today? More importantly, how do you find the style, materials, and attachment that are right for you?

WAY BACK WHEN

Sixteenth-century illustrations are the primary sources for gathering historical information about how players held stringed instruments before the advent of what we'd recognize as modern-day technique. From these pictures, we can discern two main postures: on the arm (viola da braccia); or in the case of the viol, between the knees or legs (viola da gamba). Early violins and their predecessors (the rebec and lira) were held against the left breast, or slightly higher, at the shoulder. Later they were held at the neck but with the scroll lower than the tailpiece. Even though this last position undoubtedly required some degree of firmness or steadying for higher positions and downward shifts, it is doubtful that the chin really gripped the violin.

By the 19th century, new demands on violin technique required freer use of the left hand and, therefore, more stable support for the base of the violin. In response, violinist, composer, and conductor Louis Spohr (1784–1859) invented the first chin rest around 1820. His design positioned the chin rest directly over the tailpiece. Despite this development, most players still held the violin uncomfortably against their necks with the main support coming from the left hand, which is reasonably satisfactory while playing in first position, but which impedes the flow of the left hand when changing position, especially when shifting downward.

The chin rest soon evolved from a carved wooden block (usually ebony or boxwood) clamped to the ribs, to a small crescent shape (still placed directly over the tailpiece), to more sophisticated designs placed to the left of the tailpiece for the purpose of lifting the chin clear of the violin. (Nowadays many players commonly use a shoulder rest as well).

Leading violinists in the mid-1800s, such as Pierre Baillot and Giovanni Battista Viotti, endorsed the firmer support that the chin rest provided. The device enabled violinists to hold their instruments horizontally at shoulder height and directly in front of them, while at the same time freeing up the left hand and increasing the flexibility of their bowing.

Violinists, who in pre–chin-rest times had held the left elbow much closer to the instrument than we do today, found that this new position also freed up the wrist and thumb. They had occasionally used the thumb in playing double-stops, but since they no longer needed to grip the violin neck, they placed the thumb-tip in its modern position opposite the A natural on the G string (making it far more flexible in extensions and shifting).

They made this change for a musical reason, not just for necessity or convenience. According to Leopold Mozart, elegance of phrasing was a reason for playing in positions other than first. Tonal quality and colors and varied dynamics were also potent additional motives.

TO USE OR NOT TO USE?

Despite its ergonomic and musical advantages, some players have reservations about using a chin rest. A few develop an allergy or irritation to the material used in the mechanism that connects the rest to the instrument—the clamp and screw—and as a result, several makers, such as Wittner and Götz, now offer hypoallergenic titanium screws instead of the sometimes irritating nickel-plated ones. Padded suede cushions or foam pads with adhesive backing also may help alleviate these problems (some Wolf models offer this option).

Others object to using a chin rest because it severs the connection between the oscillating sound of the violin and the player. But this line of reasoning leads to emotive arguments both for and against the use of a chin rest. The anti-chin resters feel they need to have the violin connected to them as directly as possible. Members of the pro camp contend that the instrument speaks more openly when the chin doesn't obstruct its vibrations. Since timber breathes and plastic does not, some players opt for wood, believing it aids rather than encumbers sound.

But the main argument against the chin rest is that the clamps adversely affect the tonal timbre of the violin and may damage the instrument.

TIME TO SHOP

There are about 50 different types of chin rests on the market, fashioned in a wide variety of sizes, shapes, and contours, and in materials that range from Bakelite, gel, and vulcanite to ebony, boxwood, and rosewood (listed in order of popularity), as well as a light space-age composite hypoallergenic material. Phelps Violins, a British violin dealer, includes illustrations of the many different types of chin rests on its website (www.phelps-violins.com/ accessories/chinrests.html).

How do you choose one that best suits your needs? First, take a "road test." Ask to try three or four different types at home for a week. Play descending scales, arpeggios, dominant, and diminished-seventh passages, and chromatic scales to gauge the difference in shifting with and without a rest. Record the results using the different types of rests. Ask a trusted colleague to listen for differences in timbre. (The clamps rather than the actual rest will have some bearing on the tonal result.)

The most important things in searching for a proper chin rest are comfort and fit. Make sure that your head, neck, and shoulders are relaxed and in alignment. A rest should not cause these components to be out of balance. Ideally, the nose should point straight to the scroll and the neck should be straight. And think of the chin rest as part of the overall package: Catherine Jacops at Frederick W. Oster Fine Violins in Philadelphia points out, "Keep in mind the importance of finding a good combination shoulder rest and chin rest."

TYPES & STYLES

Most violin shops carry a range of the latest styles of chin rests such as Teka, Wolf, Guarneri, Götz, and Suzuki. The most popular styles are Guarneri for over the tailpiece and Kaufmann (larger, flatter styles) for left of the tailpiece. Guarneri has a shallow, ergonomically contoured cup and is the preferred style among my professional colleagues. Ebony is the most preferred wood, followed by boxwood and lastly rosewood.

"By far the most popular [chin rest] type used by professionals is the Guarneri model," says Jim Scoggens of the Orchestra Store in Houston, Texas. "For beginning students, it would be a side-mount Dresden type."

Because of their lower cost, the most popular plastic styles among students are Dresden, Mulko, Guarneri, and Teka.

But there are other options. Wittner (www.wittner-gmbh.de) has produced the "Space Age" rest. It is allergy tested and anatomically designed with an easy-to-use, secure clip-on fitting made from the same light material. It does not require a wrench and thereby avoids damaging the instrument.

The Wolf Maestro chin rest features a skin-friendly, leather-like material that alleviates pressure. This special model can be placed to the left or right of the tailpiece or even over the tailpiece by adjusting the screw fitting. The unique Wolf screws fit six sizes from a quarter-size violin to the largest viola (www.wolfproducts.com).

Kaufmann makes a separate, soft "chin comforter" that adheres inside the cup. Other soft pads (the Chin-Chum by Meisel and Strad-Pad by the String Centre) attach easily over the rest to cover sharp edges and increase comfort.

The GelRest chin rest (available in Guarneri style only) is the most recent innovation, taking the concept of a Meisel Chin-Chum or String Centre Strad-Pad to a new level. It is a fabric-covered silicone gel pad built in to the chin rest (www.gelrest.com).

Chin rests also may come with an angle-adjustment option. For instance, the SAS chin rest comes in four heights and can be tilted within a range of about 20 degrees. If you choose a chin rest that fits over the tailpiece, be sure that it sits well and does not bear down on the tailpiece. Taller barrels can be fitted. (This is especially useful for converting violin chin rests to viola size.) Take care not to over-tighten the barrels as this can damage the ribs.

"Finding a proper chin rest can be frustrating, but it can be done," says Robert Sherman of St. Anne's Hill Violins in Dayton, Ohio. "Choose a chin rest that fits your chin and neck comfortably in your style of playing."

Many dealers and teachers alike suggest trying as many chin rests as possible, and focusing on how each one feels with your instrument and shoulder rest.

"Anything different can feel awkward at first," concludes Christopher Quinn of Quinn Violins in Minneapolis. "Only after a few minutes of playing can you be sure if a model is right."

Chin up and happy playing!

A version of this chapter originally appeared in the August/September 2004 issue of Strings *magazine.*

Contributors

Cellist **Sarah Freiberg** is a member of several Baroque ensembles, and is a founding member of the Sierra String Quartet.

Philip J. Kass is an expert, appraiser, consultant, and writer on fine classic stringed instruments and bows.

Violin maker and restorer **James N. McKean** is the author of *Commonsense Instrument Care.*

Freelance writer **Kevin McKeough** contributes regularly to the *Chicago Tribune*, *Chicago* magazine, and other publications.

Violinist **Mary Nemet** studied with Arthur Grumiaux, and has toured and recorded extensively.

Stephen Perry makes violins and operates a small music store with his wife.

James Reel covers the arts, literature, and border issues for several publications.

Violist **Heather K. Scott** is a former *Strings* associate editor who covered lutherie- and education-related issues.

Strings lutherie editor **Erin Shrader** repaired bows at David Stone Violins in Seattle before setting up her bench in San Francisco.

Cellist **Mark Summer** is a founding member of the Turtle Island Quartet, performs in a trio, and has performed and taught at several cello festivals.

David Templeton writes about people and places, music and movies, cultural trends and emerging ideas for several publications.

Former *Strings* editor **Mary Van Clay** holds a master's degree in journalism from the University of California at Berkeley.

Richard Ward is an instrument specialist at Ifshin Violins in Berkeley, California.

Index

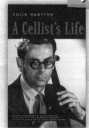

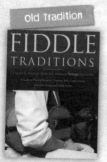